ıool

ачнеіѕ

Other titles from Bloomsbury Education

Inclusion for Primary School Teachers by Nancy Gedge

How to be an Outstanding Primary School Teacher by David Dunn

100 Ideas for Primary Teachers: Outstanding Teaching by Stephen Lockyer

Lesson Planning for Primary School Teachers

Stephen Lockyer

BLOOMSBURY

LONDON · OXFORD · NEW YORK · NEW DELHI · SYDNEY

Bloomsbury Education

An imprint of Bloomsbury Publishing Plc

50 Bedford Square	1385 Broadway
London	New York
WC1B 3DP	NY 10018
UK	USA

www.bloomsbury.com

Bloomsbury is a registered trade mark of Bloomsbury Publishing Plc

First published 2016

© Stephen Lockyer, 2016

British Library Cataloguing-in-Publication Data

A catalogue record for this book is available from the British Library.

ISBN:
PB: 9781472921130
ePub: 9781472921123
ePDF: 9781472921116

Library of Congress Cataloging-in-Publication Data

A catalog record for this book is available from the Library of Congress.

10 9 8 7 6 5 4 3 2 1

Typeset by Newgen Knowledge Works (P) Ltd., Chennai, India
Printed by CPI Group (UK) Ltd, Croydon, CR0 4YY

This book is produced using paper that is made from wood grown in managed, sustainable forests. It is natural, renewable and recyclable. The logging and manufacturing processes conform to the environmental regulations of the country of origin.

To view more of our titles please visit www.bloomsbury.com

Contents

Acknowledgements

I'd like to thank my family for supporting me in another 'bury myself away for hours at a time' task. I'm enormously grateful to all the schools who have helped me to refine my planning processes, and who have challenged the way I think about planning. My current school in particular gave me a definite reboot into just how essential learning objectives can be as a thread running through all tasks.

I would like to thank Stephen Tierney from Twitter, an inspirational head from Blackpool, whose small aside at Northern Rocks of 'don't plan lessons, plan learning' started a very reflective ball rolling in my head.

Great thanks must also go to Miriam Davey, who is one of the most patient of editors, and whose calm when I 'adjusted' her book display at the #PrimaryRocksLive conference showed enormous restraint.

Lastly, huge thanks go to my mum, who has always wanted her name in a book. Thank you, Hazel.

How to use this book

Lesson planning can provide an element of despair for even the most skilled teacher, and can cost a significant amount of our most precious resource – time.

This book will help you realise that, when done well, lesson planning can make your teaching easier, the learning infinitely better and can even save time in the process.

The book is divided into four parts influenced by the four areas of the globe: north, south, east and west. These are summarised below. Choose which area you consider you need most help with and jump straight to that section first.

Part 1. North – your curriculum base

I use the Arctic as my metaphor for the curriculum – ever-changing, but with a core of material at its centre, and with the changing landmass built around this central base.

In this section of the book, we'll look at extracting the core curriculum from a set of objectives (lesson aims for a **learning** outcome), breaking them down into tangible, workable sub-objectives, and the different ways you can add to that curriculum through careful thought and consideration.

It will help you to look firstly at what needs to be covered, and then how this can be covered in a way that reflects your interests and those of the student, including their physical environment, current affairs and popular culture. By ensuring the curriculum is made relevant to both parties, you are more enthused by your topics, and students are more engaged.

This section will also look at different aspects of planning, from digitising it to reducing it down to a workable document, rather than some unwieldy page of prose that takes far too long to decipher and use in a lesson.

At all stages, examples are given to help and guide you, and it is recommended that you read through each section, then attempt the planning with some actual objectives beside you. While the examples are useful, using an existing curriculum allows you to produce something tangible – and usable – at the end.

Like an expedition to the Arctic, planning is the key to achieving your goals. It isn't something that you should rush or think is an unnecessary evil. Done well, good planning will enable you to deliver lessons with passion, excitement and genuine intentions behind them.

Part 2. East – teaching types

The East has long been heralded as the utopia for teaching methods. Despite covering an enormous geographical area, so large as to make the assumption that 'the East has the answers' seem both egregious and assumptive, there are several lessons to take from different locations in the East – ideas that may jar with our westernised thinking, yet that let us explore the methodologies of teaching that we may have assumed to be both accurate and irrefutable. Exploring these methods, even with a Western 'eye', will help you to explore what is going on in your classroom, and even consider whether there are elements that require refining or changing completely.

This section as such is a whistle-stop tour, so links to recommended reading are included. I don't pronounce myself to be an expert in any of the methods; indeed, I am only as qualified as a very interested party who has trialled some of the methods in my own fashion. So, then, should you; read up, explore and test out the alternative thinking included in this section. You may be surprised at what you uncover about your own teaching and methods that can make a tangible difference to the learning in your classroom.

Part 3. South – planning for character

In early 1914, the polar explorer Sir Ernest Shackleton, set off on an expedition to cross the Antarctic with a hand-selected team of sailors and scientists. He'd chosen a never-before achieved challenge, but within a few weeks, his ship, The Endurance, had become trapped in the ice. Now a fight for survival, he had to lead his crew to safety – a greater challenge, which took over 20 months. Although he was recognised for saving every single life despite often quite dire circumstances, his legacy was also his dogged and quite unconventional leadership and organisational skills. Despite weeks of mind-numbing boredom on board the trapped ship, he organised and occupied the crew so fully that one commented that they barely had enough hours in the day to complete all the tasks they had to do.

There were also far fewer flare-ups than one might imagine on a ship with such close quarters. To achieve this calm, he constantly developed strategies to bond the crew together, expand their minds and let them make the most of the opportunities afforded to them.

This section of planning looks at how we can learn lessons from those extreme circumstances and sprinkle them into our planning for the greater good. The areas covered are: paired work, leadership, skill-sharing, industriousness, responsibility, teamwork and collegiality.

Can you teach character? This is a random and slightly nonsense question, yet is widely debated, especially by teachers on social media, as 'character' can be seen as the root cause of many ills in the classroom.

Take, for example, manners. You can give a perfectly decent lesson on using 'please' and 'thank you' in class, with all the children nodding sagely and giving the right answers, but the impact of that lesson will only be seen in the coming weeks if the children actually use those terms, unprompted, in their unmonitored everyday interactions. In many respects, the same can be true for everything we teach – the lesson may tick the box, but the true marking of embedded learning is if it can be drawn upon in the future.

Teaching character happens over a period of time, using a variety of techniques and skills, which this section of the book hopes to cover with in the context of planning. I believe you can influence character in the way that a trapeze artist uses a pole for balance – without this support, the trapeze artist is reliant upon their own balance, and some are more stable than others.

If this is the case, how can you plan for character in your lessons? It takes care and precision, but it is possible to build elements of character into your class life with thoughtful choices, both in an individual lesson sense and in creating a whole class culture. This culture can successfully permeate all lessons, and is well worth the initial investment in time that it may cost.

Part 4. West – planning classroom activities

The Western education system is aim-driven, but many activities within schools fill precious time with occupying tasks.

This section will unpick what an objective-led activity looks like, and how to avoid 'learning admin', where students appear on-task but are instead simply occupied. It will help you to really ascertain what activity is best for delivering your objective in as effective a manner as possible, covering many different examples.

This is about the all-singing, all-dancing section of the lesson that you get most excited about; it probably gets seen by observers, and it can be the most time-consuming section to plan. What is important is that this area – the activity – is absolutely crucial in developing learning. This cannot be understated. Any activity carried out badly becomes a bad activity – it's as simple as that.

Read on to find out what you can do about this and how you can make your activities razor-sharp (but in a blunt, infant-scissors sense).

Throughout the book there are **#proplanningtips** – information and ideas to make your planning (and teaching) a happier experience. As we know, happier teachers make happier classes.

At the end of some sections, you will find an 'In Practice' challenge – I'd encourage you to put down the book and try this task. It will help to cement the concept more effectively.

Finally, a confession. I find planning *really* hard. The tips and techniques in this book are those honed through over 16 years of teaching in a variety of year groups and settings. I hope that you find them useful, as they help me to survive!

Part 1
North – your curriculum base

Chapter 1
Unpacking objectives for a scheme of work

We all have a curriculum to follow, whether in a state, academy or independent school, and whether it's the National Curriculum or an in-house curriculum. This is the basic template of what is the minimum necessary to teach, at that age group, for that subject. I say minimum because there may be a fallacy among new teachers that this is the sum total of what we have to teach.

It is dangerous to believe that the curriculum represents all we have to teach. This is a problem with a ready-packaged curriculum plan; it will cover all the required objectives, but doesn't take into account the children in your class, the needs of the school, the learning styles your children have, or even their interest in the subject. What it does create is a generic Values curriculum with no extra flavours or nuances pertaining to your class. While the children in your class will manage on this curriculum, they're not getting a specific diet, which you as their teacher are able to bring to the table. Who wants this for their children?

The other danger, sometimes perpetuated by social media, is that there just isn't enough time to cover everything in the curriculum, let alone anything else. I firmly believe that this is inherently incorrect and something that this book will help you to realise. Think of the curriculum, where you are provided with perhaps 70% to 80% of what you could potentially cover in the class. What about that golden 20%? This is up to you and your school, and there are ways in which you can have an enriched curriculum by looking carefully at the objectives and unpacking them then repackaging them specifically for your class.

Unpacking an objective

Let's start by unpacking a typical National Curriculum objective for a subject; the example I have chosen for the purpose of this chapter is an objective from the DfE geography programmes of study:

Place knowledge
Understand geographical similarities and differences through the study of
human and physical geography of a region of the United Kingdom, a region
in a European country, and a region within North or South America.

I've chosen this objective from Key Stage 2 as it features one of the richest seams of learning: similarities and differences.

There is a huge amount to unpack from this one small objective. One of the easiest ways in which I have found to unpack something so broad is to turn it into an adjunct text – that is, a way of showing text that isn't simply prose. By doing this, you are filtering out the sub-objectives from the broader statement. Compare and contrast objectives are perfect for this.

I've turned this objective into the table below:

	Human differences	Human similarities	Physical differences	Physical similarities
UK vs Europe	A	B	C	D
Europe vs America	E	F	G	H
UK vs America	I	J	K	L

Using this table, we now have 12 areas to cover, so already we know that this will take at least 12 lessons to cover – and this is being optimistic!

I've labelled each sub-objective box with a letter to help reference it later on.

Develop objective questions

The next stage would be to create a question for each objective. This is a good way of checking that everything you plan for is set against the objectives, and gives you something to measure too. I'm going to use sub-objective A as my example to demonstrate the early stages of planning for the rest of this chapter:

What are the human geographical differences between a region of the UK and a country in Europe?

To help with this example, I'm going to use the Midlands and Turkey as my chosen locations, although the section on the Chembakolli Effect at the end of this chapter will help guide your selection for these (see page 21). With these locations in mind, our question becomes:

What are the human geographical differences between the Midlands and Turkey?

The Ella Test

The next stage in planning involves a little imagination. I call this the Ella Test. As a deputy head, I noticed that school subject leaders would have aims for the year for their subject that were sometimes only known to a few people. In order to have a real impact, I felt that the aim of a subject should be known to every single child in the school. To that end, the Ella Test was set up (and many thanks to Ella Hague, a former pupil, for being my unwitting guinea pig in this concept).

Staff were told to ensure that their overarching subject aim was so clear that anyone could ask any child in the school what a subject aim for the year was, and they'd be able to answer. This stood for children from Reception to Year 6, and was a lofty aim but one the staff and children took on board with aplomb.

So, the Ella Test for planning. I'd like you to imagine that you have taught geography to a child in your class the previous year. You happen to bump into that child and ask them, out of the blue, what the human geographical differences between the Midlands and Turkey are. In this imaginary scenario, they wouldn't run away from you in blind terror, but rather give you an answer with such recall, interest and perhaps even passion that you get goosebumps.

This is a rather unorthodox viewpoint, but one that I think distils one of the true purposes of education: long-lasting knowledge, understanding and **benefit**. The danger with teaching a curriculum to the test rather than to life is that children are canny enough to know that they only need to sustain this information for a set length of time. We steal its value as something worth retaining.

So, your 'Ella' – what might she say about your question? She might talk about the human population make-up of both locations, discussing the main industries of each, and how they are guided by the location itself. She might explain that Turkey has a strongly tourist-based economy, whereas the Midlands is built upon localised industries, and that as a result, both locations are structured quite differently. She might talk about the affluence (and poverty) of both regions, and what key differences there are between the societal structures, physical environments and buildings. She might even speak about the religion, and its influence on the population.

This all seems enormously ambitious, doesn't it? We might doubt that we could get such a salient answer from an adult, let alone a seven-year-old, but I have found one really fundamental belief to be true in all the years I've been teaching (and I look far younger than I am; I've taught for a really long time). It is this:

a rising tide lifts all boats.

You may not experience this at first when you start teaching, but it's true. Imagine the challenge of a lesson to be on a dial. At first, you might teach and hope that the students achieve the bare minimum. They do, so you crank the dial up a little more, and give them a little more challenge.

It turns out that children actually love a challenge, and sometimes the greater the challenge, the better. There is a point at which something becomes too challenging, and it is simple to identify when this occurs; it is when there is no gain in pleasure from the challenge, or when it holds little interest. If either of these two key points occur, a child's (and indeed, an adult's) brain decides it has had enough and switches off. Game over.

Research has found that when this interest is sustained, and has a specific, purposeful outcome, the sky literally is the limit. Studies into children's self-teaching strategies in the game Minecraft, for example, found that children were so keen to improve, that some ended up reading texts that were rated at an undergraduate level of understanding – how amazing is that?

Ella's response above is ambitious, but so too should your lesson objectives be. Realistic and obtainable certainly, but also ambitious and with enough 'bite' to sustain purpose and interest.

Breaking down our dream response from Ella, we can ascertain what she would need to learn in order to provide that response, put into bullet points below:

- industries and economies
- incomes
- societal structure
- accommodation
- family life
- religion.

These are of course very broad areas to explore, and they would also cover more sub-objectives than simply A in the earlier table, but they can be further focused by turning them into questions. The examples below are quite closed in nature.

- What is the main industry of X?
- Where do most people in X get their money from?
- How is life in X organised?
- What sort of houses do people in X live in?
- What is family life like in X?
- What is the main religion in X?

Some of these naturally pair up and complement each other well – for example, family life and housing – so, with judicious planning, could be taught in the same lesson.

Planning the order

The next stage in planning is developing the ordering. There are several ways to do this with a compare and contrast objective. Which of these do you think is the best method?

- learn all about the Midlands, learn all about Turkey, then compare them
- learn all about the Midlands, then compare to Turkey
- compare as you learn.

Although all three have different merits and challenges, I have found that the last strategy tends to cement what the children learn more effectively. By looking at contrasts one by one, the children are given a hook for their learning as the facts are not isolated.

With this in mind, we need to adjust our questions to take this into account. I've also reordered them, and will go on to explain why I've put them in that sequence.

- What is family life like in the Midlands and in Turkey? How similar are they?
- What sort of houses do people in the Midlands and Turkey live in? What common elements do they have, and how are they different?
- Where do most people in the Midlands and Turkey get their money from?
- What are the main industries in the Midlands and in Turkey? What are the differences and why?
- How is life in the Midlands and Turkey organised? What similarities are there, and what differences?
- What is the main religion in the Midlands and in Turkey?

I have ordered these outwards, from the known (almost all children will have experienced what could be described as family life) to the unknown (they are less likely to have a job or work in an industry, although this is becoming more common in certain areas and sectors – tourism, for example).

This ordering from the known to the unknown is key with planning. It is effectively a breadcrumb trail, leading the children from an area of familiarity to somewhere unfamiliar, but signposting the way. As you'll read in later chapters, the more familiar and relational you make the start of your journey, the longer you'll be able to sustain the interests of the children and stretch the learning opportunities.

You'll notice that the sub-objectives A and B (human similarities and differences between the Midlands and Turkey) have merged in our questions. They are best thought separately but taught together, which will be a distinction later on when the learning is planned for. It is always best to separate the objectives so that they are as simple and concise as possible, even though they may merge or alter later on; in this way, the nuances of what you are teaching become more focused.

Some of what our objectives cover also link well to the physical geography. The aspects of religion, for example, will highlight both human and physical geography. To that end, it is good to go through the same process as we did before, and then compare links between objective questions.

If we were to explore the physical differences between the Midlands and Turkey, we might end up with these objective questions:

- What is a typical home like in the Midlands and in Turkey? What do they have in common?
- What is the landscape like in the Midlands and in Turkey?
- How does the landscape have an influence on the industries and work in the Midlands and Turkey?
- How is the transportation similar in the Midlands and in Turkey? How is it different?
- Which areas in Turkey are similar to the Midlands? Which areas are most different?

This last objective stands out as an assessment investigation question. I ordered the objectives in the same way, as before, building from the known to the unknown. It would be hard to answer this last objective without the prior learning of the previous objectives taking place, so it lends itself well to being a useful assessment question. Added to that, the way it is phrased requires some comparative research skills; I haven't stated a particular area in Turkey to examine for comparison, so there is an emphasis on the students identifying somewhere themselves – which also leads them to have to justify and explain their decision-making. This is another excellent way not only of embedding their learning but also of the teacher establishing how secure their understanding is.

With the objectives for the four areas of A, B, C and D combined and ordered, you might end up with a list like this:

- Where are the Midlands? Where is Turkey?
- What is family life like in the Midlands and in Turkey? How similar are they?
- What is a typical home like in the Midlands and in Turkey? What do they have in common?
- What is the landscape like in the Midlands and in Turkey?

- What are the main industries in the Midlands and in Turkey? What are the differences and why?

- How does the landscape have an influence on the industries and work in the Midlands and in Turkey?

- Where do most people in the Midlands and Turkey get their money from?

- How is the transportation similar in the Midlands and in Turkey? How is it different?

- How is life in the Midlands and Turkey organised? What similarities are there, and what differences?

- What is the main religion in the Midlands and in Turkey?

- Which areas in Turkey are similar to the Midlands? Which areas are most different?

You may notice that some objectives have been removed or merged. Some objectives are similar and could be placed together, but they have been kept separate for a reason. There is often a disconnect with children, for example, between industry and income. Take the oil industry of Scotland as an example: the companies who extract oil operate with vast profits, yet there is real economic and social deprivation in Scotland. Examining these areas separately encourages a genuine consideration for each. I have found that putting too many objectives into one lesson aim is rather like buying a multi-functional device – it often doesn't serve as well as separate units would do.

I also added a key objective at the start: where both areas can be found. Teachers can sometimes be oblivious to the obvious, and I speak from experience. There is research into the theory of knowledge, which suggests that teachers often assume more than their students have actually learnt from them, so it is important to get the basics absolutely secure before proceeding, or you are building on very shaky foundations.

At my first school, I taught an enormously intelligent and curious girl who seemed to know an awful lot yet, at the same time, soaked up information at an incredible rate. During one activity looking at time, she became very frustrated when she was stuck on a seemingly simple question. I went to help her, and was surprised to discover she didn't know that there were 52 weeks in a year. 'You never taught me that,' she retorted. Lesson learnt! Cover the basics.

Mapping knowledge versus skills

This seems to be a perennial online debate – which is more important, and so on – but for planning, it really is a moot point. Both knowledge and skills work together in learning for almost all objectives in some way or form, so it is worth at this stage considering two key learning aspects:

- what the children need to know, or have access to, in order to answer the objective (knowledge)
- how they can locate, process and deliver that information (skills).

These work together in parallel, and it is important to consider that if you require a skill to be used by students, it needs to be either known and competently used, or explicitly taught. Too many lessons suffer from worthy intentions but with too little preparation for students, expecting them to grasp skills quickly in order to try to achieve the objective. I have found, through countless experiences, that adequate skills training more than repays itself in the long term. It may not drive the main objective forward immediately, but it ensures that you are able to deliver your lesson objectives with more confidence and success.

I have observed many lessons over the years, and two related experiences stand out for me. The first is the helplessness a teacher shows when they set a task with which the children have no familiarity, but plough on in the hope that, if they persevere, something will click. Much more resonant is the perceived bravery of teachers who halt a lesson and re-establish what to do if the class/group/individual cannot grasp the particular new skill they are expected to demonstrate. I say perceived bravery because, although I highly admire teachers who do this in an observation, it is what I would expect any good teacher would do in that situation. If you are ever in an observed lesson and things aren't going to plan (in a bad way), please do stop and recalibrate. It should be positively noted by the observer.

To ensure that the students are able to cover both the knowledge and skills basis for your questions, list them separately for each lesson. The table on the next page shows what they would be for the series of geography lessons.

Lesson	Objective	Knowledge	Skills
1	Where are the Midlands? Where is Turkey?	• Maps • Identify UK • Identify areas of UK	• Map-reading • Use of Google Maps
2	What is family life like in the Midlands and in Turkey? How similar are they?	• Midlands family life information • Turkish family life information	• Reading • Internet research • Recording information
3	What is a typical home like in the Midlands and in Turkey? What do they have in common?	• Names of rooms • Purposes of rooms	• Photo analysis • Labelling
4	What is the landscape like in the Midlands and in Turkey?	• Geographical describing terms	• Mapping • Use of Google Maps • Video analysis • Note-making skills
5	What are the main industries in the Midlands and in Turkey? What are the differences and why?	• Industries	• Research tools • Note-making skills
6	How does the landscape have an influence on the industries and work in the Midlands and in Turkey?	• Landscapes • Relationships between industry and landscape	• Mapping • Research tools • Note-making skills

7	Where do most people in the Midlands and Turkey get their money from?	• Understanding of income • Collecting data	• Research • Data analysis • Presenting information
8	How is the transportation similar in the Midlands and in Turkey? How is it different?	• Transportation types • Pros and cons of each type • Understanding of landscape	• Maps • Transportation maps of areas • Note-taking skills
9	How is life in the Midlands and Turkey organised? What similarities are there, and what differences?	• Town officials and governments	• Research • Note-taking skills • Presentation
10	What is the main religion in the Midlands and in Turkey?	• Christianity basics • Islam basics	• Comparison • Research
11	Which areas in Turkey are similar to the Midlands? Which areas are most different?	• Prior knowledge from lessons	• Research • Comparison • Presentation

A little note about thinking skills: these are valuable, but heavily dependent on your cohort, the school ethos towards teaching thinking skills explicitly, and the approaches to take in using thinking skills in a lesson.

Creating this type of table takes time but really helps you to pinpoint what you are hoping to achieve in each lesson – which is what the objectives are starting to become. In order to fill in the boxes for knowledge and skills, ask these questions for each objective stated:

- What do the children need to know, or have access to, in order to answer the objective? (knowledge)
- How can they locate, process and deliver that information? (skills)

You should recognise these from earlier. You might notice that there is some repetition in both columns. The knowledge column is still quite loose − none of the points emphasise exactly *what* knowledge will be taught (that is to come) − and with the skills column, this list might seem rather dull and bland. Again, it is the overarching aim, so will be expanded further. By creating this table when planning, you can see several elements:

- what research you will need to carry out
- what resources you will need to find or create
- what skills you will have to develop or teach.

There may already be the temptation to start planning activities for these lessons, but there are a few more planning aspects left to cover, so hold back for now. By all means come up with ideas, but avoid locking into place a task or activity just yet.

#proplanningtip: Bookmarking

For the religion objective, I quickly searched online to find out what the main religions were – I had a suspicion, but wanted to back it up. The two relevant pages (I used two tabs to compare rather than trying to remember details – a skill worth teaching in itself) I then bookmarked for later.

Bookmarking seems to be a wholly underused facility on Internet browsers. It allows you in one click to go straight to the page you recorded. In addition, bookmarks allow you to sort pages into folders, export them as a digital or printed list, and even share them with others. In this age information leads much of our online work, bookmarking can save you lots of time in locating pages you'd found previously.

Titling and goal criteria

From a planning perspective, titling is a small but crucial area. There are many schools across the UK where there is an expectation for objectives to be written down by pupils. This, as I see it, is a travesty of time-use in their lessons, and what I like to think of as 'learning admin' – events that occur in learning time but that don't progress the learning at all. Stripped down, copying the learning objective from the board into books is simply that – **copying**. We all have that one pupil (probably more) who spends half their lesson copying a statement down in their books. How is this in any way beneficial? Even three minutes copying an objective down adds up – with a four-lesson day, this adds up to 39 hours per year!

#proplanningtip: Sticky objectives

If yours is a school that insists on this practice, there is little to be done. One alternative is to have the learning objective printed onto labels so that they can be stuck into the book beforehand or afterwards. This takes a little time setting up, but saves both you and the pupils a lot of time in the long run. It is always worth asking your line manager if this could be an alternative in your classroom – the worst they can say is no!

If you are going to use the Title as a replacement for the objective, it is worth spending a little time on this area. Titling at this point is, of course, not fixed but can hone your lesson further. The idea is that you encapsulate the objective in a short and pithy statement, which can be used either as a title in their books or as the title of any resources you produce.

Some may panic at this point that they have a title but no activity – fear not! The task should be dictated by the objective and title, not the other way around, so if the task you are thinking of doesn't match the objective, should you really be using it? We cover activities later in this book, but let's nail the essentials first.

I've created the titles for our geography objectives below:

No.	Objective	Title
1	Where are the Midlands? Where is Turkey?	Where the Midlands and Turkey are
2	What is family life like in the Midlands and in Turkey? How similar are they?	Family life in two locations
3	What is a typical home like in the Midlands and in Turkey? What do they have in common?	A typical Midlands home A typical Turkish home
4	What is the landscape like in the Midlands and in Turkey?	Contrasting landscapes
5	What are the main industries in the Midlands and in Turkey? What are the differences and why?	Industries in the Midlands Industries in Turkey
6	How does the landscape have an influence on the industries and work in the Midlands and in Turkey?	How landscape generates industry
7	Where do most people in the Midlands and Turkey get their money from?	Incomes in the Midlands and Turkey
8	How is the transportation similar in the Midlands and in Turkey? How is it different?	Contrasting transportation
9	How is life in the Midlands and Turkey organised? What similarities are there, and what differences?	Midlands society Turkish society
10	What is the main religion in the Midlands and in Turkey?	Contrasting religions
11	Which areas in Turkey are similar to the Midlands? Which areas are most different?	ASSESSMENT

The key word from each objective has been used in each title. This reinforces the key words used for the lesson, and shows them spelt correctly at the top of the page. The region words are used, but scattered. Some titles have been split into two and others have a shared title (those beginning 'contrasting'). This has been done to help me clarify exactly what expectation I have of their work in that lesson.

These are admittedly quite sensible – and possibly bland – titles. Do by all means go off-piste when writing yours. Using short questions, puns, film tie-ins and portmanteaus (two words blended together) can make your lesson that little bit more memorable, as well as giving you a little smile inside. If you're no good at thinking of puns or portmanteaus, www.pungenerator.org and www.portmanteaur.com all do the job for you, with varying but often amusing degrees of success. There is, of course, an added pleasure for the class when they spot or solve the wordplay. My greatest success in this respect, was an English lesson called 'Para-Para-Paragraphs (Coldplay)' – certainly a novelty in the lesson, but I can also tell you not a single child in the class forgot how to spell 'paragraphs' after that!

Learning goals

The second stage at this point is to create learning goals: two for each objective. The first is for you as a teacher to measure the success criteria of the lesson. This I have found to be better phrased as a statement. The latter goal you will write is a self-goal – this is something the children will use to measure their own learning within the lesson. There is a growing body of research underlining the enormous value in children having self-goals to help them drive their own independent learning within a lesson, and my book *Thinking about Thinking* (see recommended reading at the back of the book) covers this in much greater detail. Put simply, this is a goal against which children can measure themselves when working in class or at home. It is the equivalent of a learning satnav when used effectively, and can form the basis of your medium-term plan (MTP), steering them back into a place where what they're doing contributes productively to their learning.

On the next page are our geography objectives, with the two goals written next to them.

No.	Objective	Success goal	Student self-goal
1	Where are the Midlands? Where is Turkey?	Children can locate the Midlands and Turkey on a map without aid.	Can I find the Midlands and Turkey without help? What clues can I use?
2	What is family life like in the Midlands and in Turkey? How similar are they?	Children can describe three key similarities between families in the Midlands and Turkey, and describe two key differences.	Am I able to describe a home life in both these areas, saying what is similar and what is different?
3	What is a typical home like in the Midlands and in Turkey? What do they have in common?	Children can compare and contrast two different homes, indicating five important features.	Can I accurately describe homes, noting what features they have in common?
4	What is the landscape like in the Midlands and in Turkey?	Children are able to describe the landscape of the Midlands and Turkey using at least four of these words: urban, structure, climate, traffic.	Am I able to look at a photograph of a landscape and identify whether it is in the Midlands or Turkey, using geographical terms?
5	What are the main industries in the Midlands and in Turkey? What are the differences and why?	Children can list the three most important industries in the Midlands and Turkey.	Do I know how these areas make money?

6	How does the landscape have an influence on the industries and work in the Midlands and in Turkey?	Children can explain how the landscape dictates the industry for a region, giving an example.	Can I connect the regions' industries to their landscapes, using an example?
7	Where do most people in the Midlands and Turkey get their money from?	Children are able to explain a typical income for someone in the Midlands and in Turkey, relating this to their industry.	Am I able to explain how someone in the Midlands earns money? Can I do the same for someone in Turkey?
8	How is the transportation similar in the Midlands and in Turkey? How is it different?	Children can list the three most common forms of transport in each area.	Do I know what sort of transport is used in each area, and why it may be different?
9	How is life in the Midlands and Turkey organised? What similarities are there, and what differences?	Children are able to explain three similarities and two differences between Midlands and Turkish society.	Can I compare and contrast the Midlands and Turkish ways of life?
10	What is the main religion in the Midlands and in Turkey?	Children can name the main religion in the Midlands and in Turkey, and any crossover there is.	Am I able to name the main religions in the Midlands and Turkey?
11	Which areas in Turkey are similar to the Midlands? Which areas are most different?	Children can demonstrate at least seven of the previous success goals in their work.	Can I demonstrate what I have learnt about the similarities and differences between the Midlands and Turkey?

You will notice that the success goals are brutally clinical – they are either yes or no, with no shades of grey allowed. Assessing the achievement of objectives from just one lesson is hard enough without having areas of doubt to manage as well. When you are marking work, but marking it against this goal in your assessment book or planner, you can either give a tick or a cross – which would require further input (and adjusted plans).

These success goals can also form the basis of your assessment piece at the end of the scheme of work. Some teachers might add some skills-based criteria, but it is best to use an end-of-unit assessment to assess the learning for that unit, based on the objectives from which these goals are derived and maintaining the thread of continuity. I have seen excellent assessment tasks in the past, carefully devised and thought-through, apart from the fact that their criteria have only the loosest connection with the weekly objectives. It is like learning the flute but being asked to play the trumpet at a grading – still reading music, still a wind instrument, but a wholly different set of skills to be demonstrating. Remember that the purpose of an end-of-unit assessment is NOT to catch the pupils out; it is to establish just how much of what you have taught has been learnt. Keep this firmly in mind.

You may think, when reading the objectives and goals as rows, that there is a lot of repetition, and also that this seems excessive. Think of this as being deliberate – when planning your activities later on, judging them against these three strands of objective really help to clarify whether the task you are asking the children to do fulfils their learning time or simply occupies it. By ensuring that we stick to meeting the objective, we are also ensuring that we stick to learning, rather than just busyness. There are few greater crimes in education than having a crafted objective and the children simply completing a shoehorned activity (one that possibly matches a few of the words, but with no discernible benefit to the children's progress). You can read more on this in the West section.

Curriculum land size

We have created our lesson objectives based on the National Curriculum, so why then is this section of planning placed in the north compass? It relates to an analogy I've grown fond of in the past few years, and concerns the size of the Arctic.

Technically, the Arctic doesn't exist, but frozen platforms roughly three metres deep do – it is the only ocean you can walk over, such is the volume of ice. A number of factors, including global warming, the season and other attributing elements, have an effect on the size of the Arctic. There is a central base of ice that generally doesn't change, but there is also an ever-changing collar of icy land surrounding this, which is constantly evolving.

If we imagine the central area as our core curriculum, then everything else is the extra we can bring to it – and bring it we must, or else we end up with what I like to call the Chembakolli Effect.

The Chembakolli Effect

Chembakolli was suggested as a place to use as a comparison location in an earlier iteration of the National Curriculum in the QCA units of study. There were sample plans to follow featuring Chembakolli, although it was indicated that this contrasting location could be anywhere.

If you don't know – and unless you are from the region or were educated during this time, you are unlikely to – Chembakolli is a region in India, and so typically quite different from the experience of most children in the UK. So far, so good.

The difficulty lay with teachers being unwilling to explore outside of this given example. Countless resources fed this, with fact sheets, books and even charities latching onto the fact that Chembakolli was being studied by thousands of children. I'm not condemning these teachers for utilising something so well resourced; I'm more saddened by the massive missed opportunity that both the children and teachers had for bringing something of themselves to the curriculum, and therefore the lesson.

When something is used as an example in a curriculum, remember – it is just that. Set it against these questions:

1. What are the reasons why it was chosen as an example?
2. What is in my children's lives that is comparable?
3. What is in my life that is comparable?
4. Can I swap the example?

This will obviously take more time than normal. You probably won't be able to use the countless resources that will have appeared online or in shops to support the example given, but what you will end up with is a more authentic curriculum, which both you and the students are able to get behind.

I read a fantastic case study a while back in the psychology book, *59 Seconds* by Richard Wiseman, regarding artists. The researchers gathered together two items from each artist – one was a commission, paid for by an enthusiast, and the other was a painting that the artist had simply created. They invited members of the public to come in and assess whether they could work out which was from the artist and which was the commission. Perhaps surprisingly, people worked out which was which correctly an incredibly high percentage of the time. The lesson from this: people can detect authenticity much more easily than we might imagine.

When considering examples for your curriculum, or any influence you have over your curriculum, make it learner-centred first and then teacher-centred. Teaching the children using resources they are familiar with, or are able to make some connection with, is incredibly valuable. They will contribute more, be more animated and engaged, and have a greater sense of ownership over it.

The first year I had to teach a contrasting location, I had two children from Japan in my class. After a little research, and conversations with them and their parents, I made Japan my contrasting locality. It made a potentially dry topic come alive. The Japanese children were enthusiastic in sharing what they knew; we had lessons with guest speakers, and even rolled our own sushi! Not only were the children enthused, but I was too. I could have played the Chembakolli card, which would have meant sitting in front of a screen researching for hours, and becoming a faux expert in the region. It would have felt fraudulent to them. Instead, my research was made face to face, with props, practical guidance and primary sources of information. Rather than taking more time, it actually took less time, and was more authentic.

It was just a small change, but it had a transformative effect on both my teaching and the children's learning. The collar of the Arctic, those little ideas and influences you have over your curriculum, are the little changes that have a big effect. Every time you accept the suggested book in the pre-printed plans, rather than making your own decision about a book you know and love, you are letting that transformative opportunity step away slightly. Of course, there are elements and aspects that we have to teach, but keep your eye out for any opportunity to forge an influence (however small) on your curriculum. It'll be worth it.

These are things to consider when looking for small changes:

- your interests
- your pupils' interests
- your school
- where you are based
- your classroom make-up
- current events
- current trends, fads and hobbies
- global news stories
- local companies and industries
- parents' jobs, interests and backgrounds.

Below are some ways in which I have used (some might suggest exploited) help from others in my plans:

- I invited a parent who was a journalist in to give a talk on how newspaper stories are constructed. She was so good, she returned every year for another four years.
- I tracked a hurricane over several weeks on a weather map.
- In one year when I ended up with an all-male class of children, I did the opposite of my advice and steered clear of anything overtly male in basis (such as football) for the influence in lessons, to try to maintain the balance of testosterone levels.
- I encouraged teachers to visit with their classes local restaurants that matched the backgrounds of the areas they were studying. Every time this has happened, the restaurants have been incredibly accommodating, and loved the chance to share their culture with the children.
- I had 15 parents cook local dishes from 15 different countries for a European food afternoon. I had to source the recipes and make a sign-up sheet outside my door, but that was it. An incredible afternoon of gorging.

- Whenever I have had the freedom of texts in English, I have considered my own passions and reading history over those recommended in the plans. To that end, I have taught speech marks using Calvin and Hobbes comic strips, and I have used bikes for non-chronological writing and Wallace and Gromit for instruction writing. The fact that I can recall them so vividly demonstrates to some extent the impact they had on me, and hopefully my past students too.

Seek out these opportunities whenever you can – the benefits really are enormous.

So why did I choose the Midlands and Turkey as my two examples in this chapter? I imagined that the class were in the Midlands and I went on holiday to Turkey in the summer. It was that simple.

So, if you were to carry out this unit of work, start with the region your children are in now as *your* Midlands. Now consider a contrasting region in Europe. Is there somewhere you know especially well? Even better, is there somewhere your class knows well? Failing that, is your town twinned with anywhere in Europe? I suggest this, because there will invariably be a twinning society, and these are normally filled with passionate enthusiasts, whom we prefer to call localised experts in this situation. Make your choice of region count; if you use the same region as everyone else, you may well be missing out on an incredible opportunity.

IN PRACTICE: I would recommend you trial this process now for a topic you have to teach in the next half term, and see how much easier it is to ensure that you are both covering the curriculum and making the lessons full, rich and challenging.

Chapter 2
The structure of your lesson

Now we have our objectives for a unit of work (you did work out your objectives, right?), we can proceed with planning our lessons.

There are many different models of lessons to plan towards, and the model I'm going to explain is the one most rigorously researched, and considered the most successful in the classroom. You may disagree with the arrangement, or may work at a school with a more prescribed set of time classifications but, once explained, I'm sure you will find it both secure and adaptable to most other models.

It is commonly known as 'direct instruction', and the lead is taken by the teacher. You can use Google Scholar to investigate it further, but be assured that with an effect size of 0.81, according to John Hattie in *Visible Learning for Teachers* it lays claim to being the most reliable model on which to base lessons. An effect size is commonly seen as the best way to judge the impact that an intervention can have against other models, and with 0.40 seen as a generally-agreed line of benefit, direct instruction holds a lot of sway.

So how does a lesson break down? It is simple − it has six distinct sections. These are:

1. Introduction/review
2. Development
3. Guided practice
4. Closure
5. Independent practice
6. Evaluation

You may have already spotted that these tie (fairly) neatly into the three point lesson, the four point lesson, the 5 Minute Lesson Plan (find out more on the Teacher Toolkit website: www.teachertoolkit. me) and so on. Nevertheless, let's take a look under the bonnet and establish just what each part is designed to do, for both you and the students.

Introduction/review

This is your typical starter. It may be a warm-up exercise, a quick introduction to new material, or a reminder of old ground that has been covered. To my mind, the first will be covered if the last two are merged and planned effectively enough. No starter worth its salt should be unconnected to the learning that follows. I also believe that, given the right environment, children are already warmed to learning. This is not a stretching of muscle groups, such as the sort you would provide at the beginning of a PE lesson; in fact, the warm-up section of a PE lesson is only of benefit if you warm up the key muscles you might use for that activity – a generalist warm-up is nice, but would not accurately serve the purpose of the lesson itself.

Instead, your starter should ground your students into a place where they can quickly establish 'this is where we were, this is what we'll do' as efficiently as possible. It shouldn't take too long and, in fact, might not even be necessary. Some teachers like to use familiar models of starters with each class or subject. Again, I would go back to the objectives and consider whether what you are laying on as a starter matches those objectives (or at least evaluates the learning that has taken place against the previous objectives). If it doesn't, should you proceed?

Development

Under direct instruction, this is almost entirely teacher-led. That is not to say you can't interact with the students – more that at this point you are the 'sage on the stage'. In John Hattie's book, *Visible Learning for Teachers*, he notes that children are adept at demonstration rather than performance. Do not be fooled, as I continually am, that a lively and interactive development session means that the children have learnt anything. Again, it should be governed by the objective, and should take children from a place of familiarity to an area of the unknown, as has been covered in Chapter 1. There needs to be a tangible connection to a context with which the children are familiar, in order to create the vital hook for them to build upon. Simply beginning a new topic to which they have no relationship at all has the potential to make them feel adrift in a sea of new information and knowledge.

Having introduced **what** the students are going to do, development is the stage when you should tell them the **how** and the **why**. This needs to be as clear and as thorough as possible – both parts. Without the why, they don't have a purpose; without the how, they don't have the direction.

Again, go back to your objective for this lesson (you should have it memorised by now), and break down in your mind how the children are going to answer that question, and why they need to. Put the question out there and give careful, thoughtful consideration to how both aspects (purpose and direction) can be resolved in the most effective manner. Don't use tasks, activities or worksheets – imagine having to do this without any student props at all. In fact, one of the best ways to practise this is to imagine having to do it over the telephone with someone. This allows you to concentrate on what you are saying and the way you are saying it, rather than your presentation of it. Sometimes for students, it may feel like they are playing a particularly loaded version of Pictionary™, with your diagrams, random words and scribbles on the board. Certainly, it might feel like that for some of my classes (but I remain a gifted artist in the eyes of many six-year-olds). With this script in mind, only use the best and most stripped-back visual resources you can, and beware of the Signal/Noise Effect.

#proplanningtip: The Signal/Noise Effect

The next time you are at a presentation, take a moment to watch the audience. Look at how their attention diverts away from the speaker when words appear on the screen. It's a natural and automatic reaction, but incredibly distracting for flow. This constant change to their attention, from listening to reading, to listening and then to reading again, can be overwhelming for some. In addition, if there are words on the screen and you have drifted from listening, you can find yourself reading them again.

Whenever possible, and if using presentation software, try instead to limit yourself to one or two words maximum per slide, plus a strong supportive image of your message or the theme. You'll get a far more engaged and attentive audience than you will otherwise. This is incredibly hard to do, I appreciate, but measure it against this question: do I want them to listen to me or read from me? Put simply, they can't do both, so decide which is the most important signal because, if you are competing, there is a danger you end up just being noise to them.

Any visuals you put on the board and any tools or devices you use, should only deepen the understanding needed to achieve the objective, especially at this point. If it doesn't directly contribute, remove it! It will distil your lesson for your students in a way that they will really benefit from.

Again, use questions for clarification of the lesson. Use them to explore both what the students know and their level of understanding from your explanation. Try to avoid using questions that evaluate their understanding of the objective so far – this has the danger of throwing your lesson off course, and is the equivalent of the waiting staff at a restaurant asking you how your meal is before you've even taken a bite!

Guided practice

This is the part of the lesson where the children demonstrate, with your help, what you want them to achieve. The emphasis is on guided with good reason – time for you to change into the 'guide at the side'. It's a fine balance – you'd hope that your earlier explanation would have been thorough enough to enable the children to take control of their learning independently, but this is very often not the case. You've shown them how to ride without stabilisers, and now it is their turn; you need to have your hand on their back, supporting and steering them.

I've found that this is the point at which most children make mistakes, and often the biggest ones too. It should be obvious that this is when feedback is the most beneficial – not in marking, but with guidance, support and words. The best lessons I have observed have been when teachers are on the ball with this – they are constantly feeding back to the students. Note that they are not doing the work for them, but pointing them in the correct direction.

#proplanningtip: Tie your hands up

In a previous book, *100 Ideas for Primary Teachers: Outstanding Teaching*, I encouraged teachers to tie up their fingers with elastic bands, to stop them from taking over physically. It is almost irresistible to do, I know, but brings little benefit to those children you are supposedly helping. If a child is finding it hard to cut out a circle, and you take over by cutting it for them, how do you expect them to improve? It stands to logical reason that the more practice they have at cutting (with guidance), the better they will get, so guide them!

#proplanningtip: Feed-forward

The level best form of feedback is so charmingly simple that it (almost) defies belief. You sit next to a child and work with them on what they are doing, talking about their decisions, narrating what they are writing and challenging them when necessary. It's intense and, if honest, impossible to do for a whole class at the same time. Nevertheless, you should strive for it in this section of the lesson as much as possible, whether working in pairs or small groups. This is the art of teaching – scanning work and giving encouragement and guidance in order that the children fulfil the needs of the lesson. You will notice incredible changes and improvements in the children with whom you do this, so try to earmark as much time as possible for it in your classroom. Your children will benefit from it, and you'll find it incredibly rewarding too.

#proplanningtip: Keep it simple (for the) students

Have the instructions for any task as simple and visibly accessible as possible. You don't want a delay to the children working if you can help it at all. They should be primed and ready to go as quickly as possible, with all the equipment they may need on their tables. I know that this seems really obvious, but sometimes there can be small delays to starting. All these do is throw the children from their focus – starting work should be their top priority, not collecting glue or sorting their coloured pencils. Hit the ground running!

This of course takes preparation. If you have a teaching assistant (TA), utilise them in doing this, preferably before the lesson starts. Where you have tables in groups, lay out one table exactly as you'd like the children to approach it to act as an example to your TA, and then there can be no doubt as to your expectations. This tip is the one that has helped me above all when managing TAs. It is a tricky task sometimes to ask someone potentially older than you, and possibly with more experience in the classroom environment, exactly what you'd like them to do, and anecdotally I know that there is very little advice given to teachers in initial teacher training (ITT) as to how to manage adults in the classroom. So use this tip: set out your stall!

Guided practice is the opportunity to hone skills that have been modelled to the students earlier, so the work won't necessarily be perfect. It is during this time that the children get to grips with their access to the knowledge and head towards their own personal goals (hereafter referred to as self-goals), so it would be worth reminding them or even introducing the self-goals to them.

Research has found that self-goals can have one of the most powerful effects on students in terms of driving their learning forwards. The self-goal allows them to keep a check on what they are doing to ensure they are sticking to the intended path. I've only recently started using these in the classroom, and they are really useful at getting students back on track in a way that 'Keep concentrating, Susan' doesn't. Zimmerman, the man who has led the most research around self-goals, calls them a strategy to make students 'masters of their own learning', which I admit I really like.

Closure

This is such an evocative phrase, and essentially sums up what a plenary should do perfectly. This is the chance to openly evaluate the learning of the lesson: looking at what has been covered, seeing what the children have achieved in their guided practice, and ensuring that they have full understanding for the independent work you are going to ask them to undertake.

It is at this point that you can address any misconceptions that the students may have in a generalist sense. It may be that you have stopped the class halfway through to clarify something; it would be helpful to cover this misconception again in the closure section. Emphasising children's incorrect thinking can point them in the right direction again, which in the long term saves valuable learning time.

I've found it helpful to see whether you can answer the objective in this section. This can be achieved via several evaluative methods, from questions to small micro-tasks or challenges that can be publicly presented. Of course, you might also assess children on the basis of their written or task work, but this is a good opportunity to measure their understanding of the skills gained and the knowledge learned in a quick manner.

The closure session should ideally be short, sharp and delivered without any panic that the bell will ring any minute. This is especially important for the next section. . .

Independent practice

Aka homework! This can, of course, be work that children produce in class but, in my experience, producing work independently is a really good measure of their individual understanding, rather than that of a collective, or that produced during a stage of learning where they can come to you as a source of information.

I experienced a 'mocksted' several years back, and while it wasn't the horrendous experience that others have perhaps had, I did get several valuable tips for better practice out of it. One of these was a total brainwave that had never occurred to me – set homework at the start of the lesson rather than at the end. Many problems with homework occur because it has been recorded badly in their books, the student has left early, or they are unsure of exactly how to proceed. I have tried wherever possible from that moment on either to have a familiar task at regular intervals each week, or to set the homework at the start or as near to the start of the lesson as possible.

There is the danger that you don't get your class to the point at which they can complete the work by the end of the lesson – that they finish the lesson with a task to do that they probably can't complete independently. Although this can happen, I've found that it happens far less than you might imagine. It is, to use a food analogy, like ordering your dessert before eating your main course – if you know you have to eat it, you are more careful consuming your main. I have found that homework set at the end of the lesson tends to be dictated a little by the pace of the lesson, your input and the students' contributions. The net result is a lowered expectation for the homework itself. If the homework sets out to allow the students to complete their own goals, then that is the best aim for you to work towards, and you'll actually move your lesson up a gear if this seems unattainable, rather than reducing the effort required by the homework.

What is the best homework, then? A task that is easy to understand (stunningly easy to understand, in fact), yet provides a challenge to complete. I would suggest that 15 minutes is a good length of time in which homework should be completed, although this is often dictated by your school's individual policies. Short and sharp, like the closure session, it should be a direct opportunity for students to demonstrate their knowledge and understanding, and should absolutely match what is needed to achieve the objective. Cutting out is not independent practice. Colouring in is not independent practice. In fact, even '15 minutes research' is not independent practice – at least, not without guidance it isn't.

Evaluation

This is the moment for you to evaluate the students' understanding and ensure that they are ready to progress. There are two schools of thought for those who are behind – keep up or catch up. I would suggest that with your objectives so carefully crafted, you can ill afford for them to be changed, unless one lesson was such a drastic fail that the whole lesson needs repeating. If you have a few children who haven't achieved what you had hoped they would in that lesson, utilise your TA to help them catch up before the next lesson. In your mind, don't accept that they have missed out on the learning; ensure that they are up to speed. You owe it to them, if your objectives build on each other (as, ideally, they should), to ensure they feel that they are absolutely on top of the topic, rather than drifting behind. Avoid letting them fall behind at all costs.

Evaluation should be simple – you look across at the success goal and, with the children's work or your notes to hand, decide whether or not they have been met. RAG it (red, orange, green) if you need to, but here is a tip – only colour in the greens. Add a dot for those who are amber. Amber children tend to have supplied work that sort of answers the question, but not completely or fully enough. It may be that you can ask them some questions in the following few days and see if they are able to supply lucid verbal replies to you. If so, 'green' them in your marking system. The red children are the ones who need a small intervention. The ideal place we want to get to is a line of clear reds or greens – no ambiguity. Have any children who have been marked as red put on the following week's plans as those who might need further clarification.

Chapter 3
Planning your lesson

Now that you have the objectives organised for the lesson, it is time to plan the lesson itself, weaving the objectives through each section as a common thread. A simple litmus test should be that, at each part of the lesson, an outside observer should be able to discern the intention – if they can't, this is a warning sign that you may have strayed too far from the objective itself.

While a 'one-size-fits-all' approach to planning doesn't work in reality, it is worthwhile considering all the stages of a lesson described previously, to see if they might lend themselves well to your topic. Although I've been teaching for a terrifying number of years now, I am still developing this myself, adjusting and refining my planning and structural practice class by class and lesson by lesson.

#proplanningtip: Doorknob Teaching

I once heard a very funny talk entitled, 'Doorknob Teaching', the concept of which is simple – you are walking to a class that you are about to teach and, even when you are touching the doorknob of the classroom door, you haven't the foggiest idea of what you are actually going to teach. As a teacher, you will experience lessons like these – days like these even (I'm looking at you, Christmas). While they are clearly far from ideal, you can also teach some of your best lessons at this point.

So what is the happy medium of planning between the six-page lesson plans you are expected to produce as a student teacher and the doorknob plan? While I think that some written planning is good for you to have, if only to share with your TA or in case of illness, what should you have in front of you when you teach a typical lesson?

#proplanningtip: Lesson plans during inspections

Those people who trumpet loudly that you are not expected to have a lesson plan during an inspection are absolutely right. With all the many things you are expected to do before an inspection, lesson plans seem to be the one thing you could possibly jettison. My question is: why on earth would you? It makes no sense at all to get rid of a piece of paper that could give your inspector more insight into what you are achieving in your classroom. In every single inspection I've had (and I've been through five), the lesson plan has made a positive difference. Given that inspectors may only be in your lesson for 25 minutes of an hour-long lesson, they might well miss the golden part that you have planned – and, just as toast tends to fall butter-side down, any inspection will miss a few of these moments. Don't ever hide your gold from the inspectors; use your plan as evidence of your work or intention in your feedback – and do press for feedback. At the very least, it will show the team your hunger to improve as a professional.

The key with a usable plan is that it should be exactly that – usable. Any font size that is so small you have to miss a beat when you read it is essentially a delaying device. The trick is to reduce the content and increase the font size until it is at a point where it becomes a necessary document to ensure you remain guided throughout the lesson.

Although I wouldn't use the 5 Minute Lesson Plan (see page 26) as an actual planning document, as a placeholder for your planning notes it hits the spot. Too many plans are filled with paragraphs of notes, written in prose, with great detailed information about what the children are going to do next.

Who is this usable plan for? If it is for you, then I would encourage you to make it far more direct and sparse, so that it supports your lesson rather than holds it up. If it is for others, such as your school leadership team (SLT), I would speak to them about the expectations of a plan during a lesson. A reasonable SLT will recognise that, while thought needs to go into a plan, word quantity does not equal quality.

Planning formats

I tend to favour the Gordon Ramsay recipe approach to planning – the objective at the top, followed by the aims of each section in verb-led bullet points. Here's a test for font size – you should be able to read it when sitting down on a chair with the plan on the floor next to you, or at 90 degrees to you on the table you are sitting next to. In essence, you should be able to glance at it to know where you are and what you are going to do next. Remember, you want to avoid having to stop the flow of the lesson to read the plan and find out where you are.

One colleague, Abbie Mann (an incredible English teacher), eschews using a written plan altogether – instead, she plans her lessons using a tried and tested PowerPoint template, with each stage of the lesson labelled on that particular slide. She is a secondary English teacher. She says that this enables her to ensure not only that all bases are covered for every lesson, but also that the students know exactly what to expect and exactly where they are in her lesson. Expectations for submitted plans are easy too; one can print off PowerPoint slides as notes, so printed plans can be supplied, if required.

#proplanningtip: Creating planning templates

Almost all word-processing programs now, from Word to Google Docs, allow you to create a template. This is a digital form to fill in, which gets rid of all the hassle of sorting out formatting, font size, etc. It can also have all your headings and categories already placed for you.

I make no bones about the act of setting up a template being a front-loaded investment – you'll need to spend some time ensuring that it is correct. After this, however, you simply need to save it as a template and then, each time you open it up, you can fill it in with the minimum of hassle. Remember, planning should be cerebral, but it shouldn't be time-intensive or arduous.

For those who really want to automate their planning, I would explore the power of mail merge. This involves three documents: your planning template, a table with all your plans in and a third document, which is created by the first two. I have used this method for a few years now, and will happily admit to doing it in this way for one reason only – laziness.

I can't bear the thought of cutting and pasting my objectives several times, let alone typing them out again, so I organise myself digitally. I create my medium-term plan in the table document shown in Chapter 1 (see pages 18–19). I then fill in other key lesson-specific details in this table, press one button (it really is that simple), and a set of plans, complete with all the details I want, is produced.

So here's a rule of thumb – anyone who is spending more than ten minutes writing out their plans onto paper really would be better off using one of the digital methods explained above and typing it out. I promise it will save you time in the long run!

Some schools will have very prescribed plans to hand in for evaluative or checking purposes. If these are essential, try to ensure that the plan works for you as much as possible, rather than for your leaders. This may seem rebellious, but if you ask for the primary purpose of the plan and they explain that it is to help guide you as a teacher, they have little wriggle room for you to request that it then serves you.

Forward-thinking schools might ask for retrospective plans. These can be quite a relief to produce (I tended to cut and paste my medium-term plan, with an evaluation section added), and can also help you the following year – especially if you make careful notes on the plans about what worked and what didn't work, and how you might have addressed that lesson in a different way. A year can be a long time in school, so reading over last year's lesson evaluations can nudge your thinking about what to improve.

One example of brilliant planning that I saw was made by someone who had nailed their support for plans for subsequent years, but it also required the dedication of someone who would happily describe themselves as 'quite anal' about paperwork, bordering on OCD. She had a folder with clear plastic pockets inside, each complete with a sticky label on it detailing the topic and the week of that unit of work. Inside were any necessary worksheets or resources, the plan itself and (here is the gold) a colour copy of some completed work. This was a stroke of genius. Not only was there clear, categorised evidence of that plan at work, but there was also an example, indicating expectation, for the students to look at to ensure they were on the right track with their work. I couldn't begin to organise myself enough to do this, but I thought it was a very clever development of planning, and one that I would encourage, either analogue (folder) or digitally (online).

If you really want to save some time, Bloomsbury have put two of these plans online for you to download – please follow this link: www.bloomsbury.com/lockyer-lesson-planning.

Questions

Questions, I believe, are part of the lifeblood of any good plan. Some plans make explicit use of this, italicising them to make them more visible, and in *Teach Like a Champion*, Doug Lemov notes that some of the most successful teachers he witnessed in preparing for his book wrote down the questions they were to ask the students in their care.

I concur with this concept, and would encourage those planning to also write the questions they may ask. In my book *Hands Up* I estimate that teachers ask up to 400 questions a day to students, yet we answer many of them ourselves. To allay this in some way, I recommend some form of public punishment for teachers, shared with students. Instead, writing five questions for each lesson you teach, each with a purpose of either driving the learning and thinking forwards or of being used as an evaluative measure for student learning, can be a good way of ensuring that your questions remain focused and purposeful.

I would also be inclined to highlight questions in your plans, perhaps even with colours to note which are general questions for the whole class to consider and which are evaluative questions for a specific subset of your students. Highlighting like this enables you as a teacher to find them quickly in your plans, as well as reminding you that they are there to be asked. Try it for one lesson just to see how powerful a teaching intervention this strategy is.

Sharing plans

Sharing your plan with others in your classroom is incredibly helpful, and we need to get over the almost English shyness or humility involved in this practice. Too few teachers are comfortable with sharing their plans with other adults in the classroom, but what is the alternative? Without sharing plans, you are asking adults to guess your intentions, picking these up as the lesson progresses – and no more debilitating a procedure could occur for someone who is a learning ally.

Instead, share your plan with any TA or volunteer. Remain with them while they read it (remember, it shouldn't take too long to read), and if it isn't noted in the plans themselves, talk them through what you'd like them to do at each stage of the lesson. Quite a few teachers become frustrated at the lack of impetus TAs sometimes offer lessons, so this is the perfect way to address this, using professional dialogue and a written back-up as an aid for you.

If you can, store your past plans, attaching any resources to them. Note on the plans the aspects that went well, as well as the things you would adjust next time you take that particular lesson. Our colleagues in secondary tend to have the ability to repeat the same lesson with several sets, whereas ours are one-offs. Having worked in both sectors, I know that the second lesson I taught with the same content was better than the first in almost all cases, so make a note of the changes you would make for next time. Even better, adjust the plan digitally, so that when you revisit it, the changes are already made. You may think you'll remember, but given that a primary teacher can take almost 2,000 lessons in one year, this is less than guaranteed

#proplanningtip: Onedoc

As I said in the introduction, I'm not the biggest fan of planning, and can also be deeply creative (read, disorganised) with computer files. To that end, I have started Onedoc planning. Under my weekly plans for a subject, I have all the resources that may be used for those lessons – images, slides, worksheets, web links – all in one document. What I've noticed is, by doing this, I have far less filing to do and everything for that lesson is under one roof, so to speak. This may seem terrifyingly obvious to many readers, but for someone who has taught for 264 years, it has been revolutionary for me. Try it!.

Part 2
East – teaching types

Chapter 4
Shanghai maths –
for all subjects

Unless you've been under a rock, you won't have been able to avoid the term Shanghai maths in recent years. Seen by some as a panacea to teaching mathematics, it is in reality a fairly simple structural procedure for introducing ideas. Broken down into its most simple framework, it takes a concept through three distinct stages:

- concrete
- pictorial
- abstract.

It is easiest to explain this by way of an example. Let's imagine that your aim of the lesson is to demonstrate that you can combine halves to form whole units – a simple aim for Year 1, which can create much confusion, I assure you.

You start by presenting the class with two oranges cut in half. You establish with the class that the oranges have been cut in half. This is the **concrete** stage – a place where they can see the maths in real life. With the class, you put two halves together and make a whole unit – one orange.

Next, you bring up a visual representation of four semicircles. Moving them together, you place two semicircles next to each other to form a perfect circle and demonstrate again, using a **pictorial** visual, that two halves make a whole unit. You might do this several times over with different half shapes brought together, to indicate that two halves together make a whole unit.

Finally, you write ½ + ½ on the board. This is the **abstract**. You ask the children to complete the sum by working it out. You might then write 1 ½ + ½ on the board, and ask them to relate this to the concrete and then pictorial to solve the problem.

It is so simple a method, and yet has revolutionised much of the maths teaching in Shanghai and further afield, hence its celebratory aura. I think it chimes most well with us in the West because, in our need to complete objectives, we can sometimes make a false assumption that students will join the dots for themselves. Most times, of course, it is easier to join the dots looking backwards rather than forwards, and the first stage, showing the concrete, can be lost.

If we think back to one central aspect of planning – to draw the unknown from the known (see page 8) – we can see why this method might be especially powerful. Using a concrete example allows us to establish the known quality for our students.

I think that the pictorial and abstract are incredibly well served in our classrooms. One of the most powerful tools I have seen in recent years in primary classrooms is Numicon (a set of plastic shapes with corresponding holes for values), and I rue the day I didn't come up with something so effective yet easy to produce, such is its use in our classrooms. It is, however, a pictorial tool – and one that should be celebrated. It doesn't, however, replace the need for a concrete, real-life tool to explain mathematics – nothing but reality does. An easy measure for 'Is this concrete for the children?' can be tested by simply asking the second question: 'Do my children use this in real life?'

Any teacher who has used a craze or fad in helping children to understand a foreign or unknown concept will attest to this. Take Gogos Crazy Bones (tiny, alien-like toys), for example. When these came about, I jumped on board quickly, using them to help with sorting and division problems. I used their colouring to build real-life bar graphs (thanks to the help of some Blu-Tack™ and photographs), and the children I taught were completely hooked. They found the maths we were covering relatable because I was utilising the very items in their pockets. You can't measure the excitement you bring to the classroom when you utilise what they play with at break time.

With every maths lesson you teach, try your hardest to bring something of the real world, the concrete, into the start of that lesson. Take them from the known to the unknown. This takes real care and planning, but the journey you take the children on becomes so much more relatable to them, as they can track back through your lesson to a point to which they feel comfortable in relating, and move forwards again with this in mind.

I think the most damaging aspect of Shanghai maths is that second word. Taking the word 'maths' away from the concept, this idea of leading from the concrete to the abstract can be applied to almost any subject in our primary curriculum, bringing benefits to us all.

To an extent, this does happen. In art, we give children items to draw and copy as muses for their work. In history, we talk about using primary sources as a key way in for the children (although this does leave us in an area of an introduced 'known' rather than an evolved 'known'). But, to my mind, it is often seen for many subjects as an optional extra, rather than a very tangible part of their learning.

IN PRACTICE: Consider the next three lessons you have to teach. Which boxes could you genuinely tick? Write your answers – what you will use – in the gaps below:

	Lesson 1	Lesson 2	Lesson 3
Concrete			
Pictorial			
Abstract			

It's harder than you might think. Consider this though: if it is hard for you to make links backwards or forwards, how much harder must it be for your pupils, without the wealth of experience that age and professional training bring?

I prefer instead to think of it as **Shanghai connections** – making connections to help form abstract ideas as something more tangible for students. For any gaps left in the table above, try your hardest to fill these in, and then use them in your lessons. See what a difference they make to the understanding your students have and their connectivity between concepts. When in doubt, relate it to the first time your students are likely to come across that concept in their day-to-day lives, and use that as the example.

I'd also encourage tangible, physical examples whenever possible. I once taught a series of lessons on fractions using food (a regular theme for me), and studiously recorded photographs of the fractions I made using fruit, biscuits and hot cross buns. When I used them with a later class, they could have really been anything – their 2D-rendering reduced their effectiveness dramatically. I'd lost any excitement that the real-life items had brought to the lesson. That wasn't to say I wouldn't use them; rather, that their power had diminished.

Chapter 5
Bansho board work

This is a method of teaching that was developed in Japan, with sadly no direct translation to English.

The concept is really easily explained in a diagram, below:

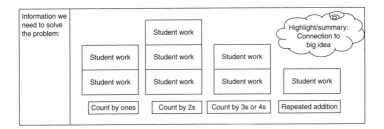

As the title suggests, it involves a very wide whiteboard, the wider the better. With the advent of interactive whiteboards, or IWBs as they are sometimes referred to, the size of the classroom board has diminished to a smaller landscape rectangle. The oncost of this, combined with a slide- and graphics-led input from teachers, is that anything that's on the board doesn't stay on it for very long. How can it be that something is important to share with students, yet gets removed far more quickly from their sight than perhaps is helpful for them?

#proplanningtip: Set-up

For those who already have a wide board – and two widths of an ordinary IWB are ideal for Bansho – you have little to prepare for this teaching method at the moment. For those without, see if you can have the maintenance department put an ordinary whiteboard next to your IWB. I've found this ideally to be to the right of the IWB as you face it, but I am a left-handed teacher so this may simply be my personal preference.

If you can't stretch to this, I have also found Magic Whiteboard to be a keen substitute. This is statically charged plastic sheeting that can be placed on almost any surface, and which can be written on and wiped off with ordinary board pens. It is cheaper to buy on popular auction sites than direct. I have found it so useful, in fact, that I placed it on the top of my IWB surface at my old school, so that I could make notes on the main board without turning the projector on.

With your set-up complete, some explanation is needed as to how this method works. It originates from mathematical teaching, specifically problem-solving techniques. The teacher explains the stages of the problem across the top half of the board, with notes and moving from left to right. At each stage, students are invited up to contribute underneath the teacher's examples. When the problem has been fully explained and solved, in front of the students is a clearly staged and staggered example of how to solve that type of problem. With this example visible, students are then asked to solve similar problems of their own in their books.

I first came across Bansho board work through researching problem-solving teaching online. I was immediately captured by the permanency of the teacher's notes, essential for detailing the different stages of problem-solving. I knew that, in previous lessons, I had generated up to nine different written slides to cover these stages, and became instantly aware that what I was doing was asking the children in lessons to both learn and memorise the techniques, two distinct skills that aren't well paired together.

The difference with using this method is truly transformative. Some teachers might view this as 'recipe teaching', where the students are guided every step of the way, but I think the way in which Bansho differs is that it has the children's examples underneath – they are cooking themselves at every stage. They also have a clear reference point should they get stuck at any stage in their own work. The ability to move back to a point with which they are familiar (from the unknown to the known again) is key, as it helps to embed their thinking through being able to compare the method on the board to the method in their book. It is offered guidance rather than hand-holding.

I have experimented with children solving their problems in the same way as on the board but in their books, and did not find it worked particularly successfully. The children became frustrated that they might have to write sections of the problems out repeatedly, and they were also very poor at estimating how much space to use (rather like long titles and the infamous 'bubble writing'). You might find, however, that you can make a written Bansho work for you.

Rather like Shanghai maths, I feel that Bansho lends itself well to many, if not all, subjects. In fact, the two merge together almost seamlessly. It is the board equivalent to instructions for a paper aeroplane and, as a methodology, ties in with the lesson plan of direct instruction explained in Chapter 2 of this book (see page 25).

To use this for other subjects, consider the stages of learning through which you will take the students from the known to the unknown, and then place these on a grid from left to right. Underneath would be the section where they would write what they are doing at each stage of the explanation. This is really useful for you as a teacher to ensure that they are listening and following your explanation carefully. It allows you (with a broad stroke – remember, it is just one student's perspective) to see that they have grasped every stage of your detailed explanation. This in turn allows you to correct misconceptions at the very best time – at the point of discovery.

IN PRACTICE: Consider the three objectives indicated below, and how you might put these into a Bansho order for your board.

Recognise the difference between landlocked and water locked countries					
Explain how impressionism differs from naturalism					
Identify the times when you would start a new paragraph					

I've clearly shown some very tough examples there, which might require three different approaches to simply building on a previous stage, such as the traditional Bansho model. This is done deliberately, to help indicate how you might use the Bansho approach for three potentially testing challenges.

It is interesting to consider how each of these objectives might be taught without using the Bansho method. Perhaps the children would pore over atlases for the first (with all the exciting distraction this brings)? For the second, perhaps two slides, shown one after the other, with the teacher commenting on each? For the last, maybe a range of text examples, indicating where breaks should be made? Compare this to a Bansho approach.

For the waterlocked and landlocked objective, this is a simple procedural technique: identify a country, identify its borders, and look around the borderline to see whether it is connected to countries or water. Here, then, are your stages, just set out horizontally. If I were to teach this lesson, I might use four pictures of countries for the teacher and pupil sections, and use arrows and annotation as my notes, the pupils doing the same. They would end up with something akin to a spotter's guide to countries on the board. One way to extend this idea would be to cover over your notes on the board with sticky notes near the end of the lesson, and see whether the students can identify what was underneath using the cues around the board.

For a compare and contrast task, such as the art objective, I'd again use pictures. I'd start with one they know (I'll assume here naturalism) and have them point out features, and then in the second stage use an impressionist picture and do the same with the features. Placing these pictures again in stages three and four, I'd ask the children to identify differences, and then have a fifth picture shown to see whether they can not only explain which style it is in, but *why*. The pupil contributions could be repeated with different pictures. Again, they would have a large display showing the methodology they need to identify similarities (compare) and differences (contrast) between the two styles.

For the paragraphing example, I might break the format to my needs a little and instead of five built-upon stages, place five texts in each stage, each with a hidden example of when a paragraph break is required. I would still follow the 'known to unknown' pattern, moving from the most familiar rule for the children to the least familiar. In the pupil section, I would have some more simple text, each illustrating a key paragraph-break rule.

Granted, preparing a Bansho board session might take a little longer, but these examples will go some way to explaining the enormous difference they can make in understanding for your children.

Chapter 6
Wabi Sabi

This is a philosophy rather than a teaching method, but jars with Western thinking on beauty. Although the literal translation does nothing to help us understand this concept, the philosophy bases itself on three central beliefs:

- nothing is perfect
- nothing is permanent
- nothing is complete

This may seem highly negative, but the philosophy looks at the charm and beauty of imperfection, impermanence and the incomplete. Indeed, these are celebrated in Japanese culture, at odds with the Western belief that perfection and completion can be achieved and should be admired as such (this is derived from Greek philosophies).

How does this have relevance to teaching in the UK, particularly planning? When I first came across the term, 'Wabi Sabi', it was from some work that I was doing with a Year 4 group, where we were writing about the beauty of decay. I had found a website filled with pictures of abandoned buildings, and found a delight in nature 'taking back' its land by growing trees in the middle of rooms, birds nesting in rotting wooden staircases and moss growing like hungry stains along the walls of old hospitals. These were an unusual muse, designed to encourage creative writing about the juxtaposition of something natural and something man-made, and Wabi Sabi came up in my research.

This is not to encourage imperfection in work, but rather to accept it, and know what to do next. We can fear imperfection to the point that it inhibits us from beginning some tasks, and I'd imagine a great deal of students often experience the very same. Adopting this philosophy, perhaps by adjusting it to say 'nothing is perfect, finished or permanent', changes the mindset of children from one where there is a defined work in mind as a goal to one where everything can be adjusted, improved and polished. You will rarely find a composer, singer or writer who submits their work because it is complete; rather, they can do no more to get it to the point to which they'd like to reach.

Having this philosophy in your classroom helps students to acknowledge that there is always something that they can refine in their work. I live in dread of another experience like the *one* time I taught in Reception for an afternoon. Despite having worked in Year 2 for over a year, I was still nervous of this complete change, so I planned quite a number of activities. They were all complete within around half an hour, the cry of 'done' echoing in my ears. Wabi Sabi aims to eliminate this concept of 'done', changing it to 'done, so far'.

IN PRACTICE: No plan you write will hit every single base you attempt to cover, so accept this and, instead, use Wabi Sabi to reflect on each plan and each teaching experience you have. Ask yourself:

- What could I change to improve that lesson?
- How could I ensure that the students' work is more complete and rounded?
- What could I do to make students' learning more permanent from that session?

These three questions are all you essentially need to evaluate your lesson. The boundaries between your teaching and children's learning flow together, and the answers you give should feed into a more responsive and reflective lesson next time. Try, where possible, to write down your answers or annotate your plan (either physically or digitally) so that the next time you use it, you will recognise your own learning.

#proplanningtip: Reflecting on your planning

Social media tools can be brilliant for seeking other perspectives. I asked teachers on Twitter what questions they would ask to reflect and evaluate their planning, and the response was really interesting, including:

- How could you improve the promotion of student learning habits?
- How could you deepen the learning – stretch and challenge?
- What was the best part of that lesson?
- What actions did YOU take to achieve it?
- How can you deliberately replicate it?
- What positive and negative influences did your pacing of the lesson have on the children's learning?

Thank you to @BetterMaths, @nancygedge, @Sue_Cowley and @Miss_J_Hart for these suggestions.

Planning complacency

Wabi Sabi also tackles the area of planning complacency. We might view using a good plan again as efficiency, but consider what differences there are between the class you first used that plan with and the current class:

- cohort
- make-up
- gender
- school
- environment
- class culture
- previous history.

All these are likely to be either slightly or significantly different to the last time you taught the lesson, so consider each of these factors in turn and reflect on how they might adjust your lesson for the better. Remember, we aren't seeking perfection; we are looking to ensure that our plan is on the pathway to perfection.

Chapter 7
Lesson study

This has grown in interest and popularity in the UK in the past few years, thanks mainly to the work of Dr Pete Dudley and David Weston. It is suggested that it has actually been used as a pedagogical method of professional development for more than 140 years in Japanese classrooms, and uses honest discussion, clear focus and a healthy dose of collegiality.

The concept is simple. Three teachers plan a lesson together, focusing on one simple teaching objective (that is, format of teaching, not content). This lesson is then taught, with two of the teachers observing against that one objective, not against the lesson or teacher as a whole. The lesson objective is then evaluated, refined and redrafted if necessary, and repeated by another teacher.

This is, of course, the summary of one method put into a paragraph, and it cannot do this concept justice! I would highly recommend you read Dr Dudley's 'Lesson Study Development', or his free handbook *Lesson Study*, the link for which can be found in the References and recommended reading section at the back of the book (see page 106).

The professional distance that this type of observation produces is fantastic, and one of the reasons for its growth in the UK. Any profession that is vocational makes an emotive link between the task and the person. This is why observations can often become very charged and emotionally fraught. By letting the focus remain on one specific area, and having all the observers as stakeholders, this reduces the emotion of the event to one of collegiality (provided there is trust in the relationship). Framing any conversation as professional dialogue, and ensuring that the areas discussed focus exclusively on the pedagogy in question, allows honest discussions to ensue.

Collaborative planning

What is particularly interesting is the collective planning aspect of lesson study. Consider some of the ways we 'plan together':

- one person plans a subject and shares these plans with others, who follow
- scheme is borrowed and followed
- one person writes their own plans.

When viewed like this, planning seems quite isolated, doesn't it? It allows only the strengths of the planners themselves to come through in the written plan. Through experience, I know that the same plan can be taught in three entirely different ways by three teachers, each bringing their own skills, experience and personality to the plan. How, then, are these refinements shared except by discussion afterwards – and when the moment is essentially lost?

Planning together shouldn't be a complicit acceptance of a plan given to you. It should ideally be like the 'pot luck' meal in America, with everyone bringing something to share. Here instead is a format, based around lesson study, which I am shoehorning into the term 'planning study'.

Decide at the outset one key factor that should influence the planning process. Here are some suggestions, although ideally this should come from either the planning team honestly appraising their own areas of planning development or the school development plan (SDP).

- What can we do to ensure greater progress?
- How can we improve assessment within the lesson?
- How can we encourage greater lesson involvement from girls?
- How can we help students to retain their knowledge more effectively?

As a team, examine the objective against the planning study aim. Brainstorm opportunities to address the planning study aim through this lesson objective. Keep this list available, and with the flexibility to be added to at any point in the process.

Examine each stage of the lesson with this planning study in mind (perhaps using the direct instruction model of lessons as a guide, see

Chapter 2, page 25). Looking at each stage, everyone contributes suggestions, building a plan that addresses both the objective (primary purpose) and the planning study aim (secondary purpose). In the plan, highlight direct contributions to this aim.

Separately teach the lesson. This is where the planning study model differs from Lesson Study. While the idea of the latter is laudable, it is very time-intensive, requiring three teachers to have non-contact time for three periods of time each lesson (planning, execution, evaluation). Planning study still requires meeting time before and after the lesson itself, but produces less timetabling strain.

Regroup after the lesson has been taught, and evaluate the planning study aim for each section of everyone's lesson, against the following criteria:

- Was the aim achieved?
- How was it achieved?
- What was the measure of success used?
- What influence will this have on future lessons?

The key is to disseminate the findings really simply to all teaching staff and SLT. This can be done by distributing the plan, annotated with findings and changes and with the planning study aim emboldened at the very top. In order for all the school stakeholders to benefit from the study, the results and findings need to be shared as quickly as possible, and in a format that is easy to identify and interpret.

#proplanningtip: Why are we so nervous to share our plans?

It is hard to ascertain whether this is a uniquely British sensibility or not, but anecdotally I know of only a few really exceptional teachers who are comfortable sharing their lesson plans. This is really unusual, but highlights both a fear of judgement about their plan and how highly personal plans end up being for teachers. A good plan will share personality, nuance and the individuality of a teacher. I find it refreshing when I see something on a plan that I wouldn't normally attempt to try in a classroom, as it forces me to consider why it wouldn't work for me or why I would be resistant to using it in the first place. It seems that we are far happier sharing resources and ideas from our classroom (many of which are shared online using the excellent #pedagoofriday hashtag) than our plans themselves.

We should instead treat them as Volvo did when it designed the best mechanism for locking a seatbelt in a collision. Rather than holding the patent for this and profiting from it, Volvo decided to make this free to use, knowing that this decision would lead to thousands of lives eventually being saved.

Good plans deserve to be shared, celebrated and explored – plundered, even, for ideas and direction. Any professional critique of a shared plan should acknowledge the personal step that a teacher has made by being willing to share their plan with others.

It would be lovely to hear of any teachers willing to share their planning study explorations, and I would be delighted to accept any submissions to mr.lockyer@gmail.com. Alternatively, share these online using #PlanningStudy as an accompanying hashtag.

Part 3
South – planning for character

Chapter 8
Paired work

One strategy developed by Shackleton seems to have been largely ignored decades after its benefits became apparent – that of rotational pairing. The base principle was simple enough – boredom sets in when you have to do the same task repeatedly, and working with the same person all the time can produce great bonds, but also drive feelings of isolation, carrying an unfair workload and exclusivity. Shackleton recognised that these small but natural human traits could tear his team apart, so he spent careful time organising this so that it was almost impossible for it to occur.

Consider six children and three jobs you need them to do. If each child were assigned a different letter, you might see the task sheet as looking like this:

Job 1	Job 2	Job 3
A + B	C + D	E + F

This makes perfect sense, perhaps with the danger that they might get bored of their job, so you might rotate them after a while.

Shackleton felt that this didn't help them out at all. Instead, he would have seen this as a waste of forging and cultivating strong generalist bonds. He would have probably organised it as follows.

With six people, there are 15 combinations to make: A + B, A + C, A + D, etc. Shared among three jobs, this would last five days, with each person working with everyone else at least once. But in order to give them variety, he would have rotated the jobs regularly too, leading to 15 days of variety for everyone, before starting again! The same idea as above, but pimped!

The benefit is that this can bring a class of 30 children far more variety of dialogue, even in paired seating and speaking. With a class of 30, and some judicious planning beforehand, you can enable each child to sit next to or work with another child for 29 different occasions before they pair up again, so if you did that all year, you might have one child working with another child for six full days.

This can help the dynamism of your class in a multitude of ways. Firstly, it rids the challenge of 'no one wants to work with Brian', sadly far too common in some classes. By spreading the social load, it can allow each child to build a working relationship much more effectively than any other system.

It also neatly curtails friendship challenges. I can't find a single secondary school that allows children to opt to sit next to their friends, yet we sometimes allow it in primary. By using a rotational partner system like this, you can let them sit with each of their friends, and everyone else, over the course of the year.

Keeping track of this is easy – you just need to make a cipher wheel to organise partners. These were used in the past as a device for codes that were fairly simple to break but worked perfectly. A link to a set of instructions for making a letter version can be found in the online resources for the book, at www.bloomsbury.com/lockyer-lesson-planning.

Make your own, by designing a cipher wheel and having your class names around the rim of both circles. Put a dot on the inner rim at the first name you wrote. That shows your first pairing. Each day, rotate the outer dial by one name, and you'll have a perfect system for rotating pairings. To help you remember, I'd write the dotted pairing in your daily diary. If you put a complete revolution in at a time, you'll only have to do this seven times throughout the year, and yet you'll still end up with an enormous variety for pairing.

#proplanningtip: Talk partners

A favourite in primary school, make sure children earn their keep. In many observations, I have seen talk partners used as a filler rather than as a depth-learning activity. The best talk partner activities get the pairing to reach a mutual conclusion to a question or puzzle, but in a way that requires both their inputs.

There's a simple rule of thumb to measure whether a talk partner is worth using or not; if the children could come up with the same answer on their own, let them. If the answer can be improved by sharing ideas with other children, use talk partners.

Chapter 9
Leadership

An experiment for you in your classroom: with the children listening, say that you are looking for a leader with a very particular set of skills (note, you aren't going to find them and kill them, Liam Neeson fans). Watch the physical change that occurs as you are saying these words; spines are straightened, eye contact increases, faces engage. If these are the physical differences, what then are the mental differences that leadership and responsibility bring to children?

Building opportunities for leadership in your lessons is something that reaps huge rewards in both your teaching and the children's learning, some of which won't necessarily be visible straight away.

The advantage of this is that leadership skills can be built, refined and developed from an incredibly early age – I would say from three upwards. Giving a young child responsibility, even in some small gesture, has an impact on them and the others in their class. It encourages maturity, can ease the life of the teacher, and helps to encourage children to build positive models of beneficial hierarchical structures (it lets them know that sometimes it's good to have a leader).

Leadership can be built into lessons with ease. Consider all the tasks you need to complete yourself, and the tasks needing completion by the students. The leadership roles should emerge under one or more of the following areas:

- administration
- personal growth
- mastery.

Administration

There is a multitude of small admin tasks needing fulfilment by students every day in a classroom, from giving out equipment to collecting in work. The difference between 'doing a job' and the leadership of that task is how you package it. If you ask the same child to give out scissors in a practical task, that is a job. Asking them to manage, store and look after scissors, ensuring that they are all collected in, becomes management. Knowing that they will do this role well, and can help others who find cutting a challenge, becomes leadership.

Build a role for leadership and it gives you one less precious thing to consider in your day-to-day management of the classroom. Children especially love the responsibility of this, so really do consider the many admin tasks you complete each day that could be easily handed over to a child.

At one school I worked in, the house points were collected each week. This was quite boring and laborious and, because it was a Tuesday morning requirement, straight after morning briefing, I often forgot it. My solution was to have a student lead it. It was much more of a weight from my mind than I first considered, and he did brilliantly, carrying out this task without prompting every Tuesday. Another key detail in his success was that, very quickly, the children in the class knew not to speak to me about any house-point issues, as I would always direct them to him.

Personal growth

Some leadership roles in your classroom you will give out to a child who needs the type of bolstering that having a role can give a child. This is admirable, but must be handled with care. Start by pairing them with another child who will be supportive and not inclined to take over the job on their behalf! Having them write out their job descriptions (yes, genuinely) can also help to give them a really clear idea of what you are asking them to lead in the classroom. The gains in responsibility through leadership are enormously empowering, so think carefully about a task that you know the child in question will be able to succeed in quickly, albeit with some effort put in. The aim should always be to both empower them and get to the next stage.

Mastery

This is for children who show a real aptitude for a specific task, and is designed to allow them to share this skill with others around them. These are children who you have noticed demonstrate a mastery over a specific skill, technique or practice in the classroom (or outdoors). Consider a leadership role for them, and speak to them about how they could take this on as a role in the classroom.

The best example of this is that of the digital leader. A new initiative in the UK, these are students who show an interest in technology and computing, and the role was utilised to help other pupils and teachers. It has gained a life of its own, and many schools have digital leaders working in a variety of roles; they even have their own conferences and online chats!

The aim of any leadership role should be to build up the student and reduce your workload, so select and manage leadership roles carefully. The role should be empowering, not debilitating. Review the roles regularly, and don't forget to mention them in school reports and to parents when you get the chance (ask the children their favourite jobs when writing their reports).

Chapter 10
Class values

Having an umbrella philosophy for your class can help to guide the wider picture of lessons, learning and culture in ways that would surprise you. I'm not talking here about class rules or charters, although they have their place. I'm thinking more about mini mission statements – values that you agree as a class to strive towards or live by.

I first became interested in mission statements when I read those of Zappos, an American shoe company with an incredible reputation for customer service. Have a read:

1. Deliver WOW Through Service

2. Embrace and Drive Change

3. Create Fun and A Little Weirdness

4. Be Adventurous, Creative, and Open-Minded

5. Pursue Growth and Learning

6. Build Open and Honest Relationships With Communication

7. Build a Positive Team and Family Spirit

8. Do More With Less

9. Be Passionate and Determined

10. Be Humble

Don't they read well? Which could you use for your class? Forced to pick one, which would you choose?

Let's explore this a little further. I've randomly chosen number nine on the list, as it most suits my current class. I'd change the phrasing to: 'We are passionate and determined' to begin with, as this includes us all. Children are sponges for culture, and if we model our core value, children will identify and replicate it (it really is almost that simple).

I'd begin by showing this phrase at the start of the year and taking examples of what this means from the children. Get defined ideas and really emphasise the verbs of any statements they make. Next, I'd place it at the top of my plans, as a nudge to remember it in my planning and in all I do. I'd ensure that I used the words 'passionate' and 'determined' in the marking of every person's book in the first few weeks. I'd use the terms at the start of a lesson to emphasise how they relate to learning and expectations. I'd use them again at the end, highlighting how a certain person or piece of work had encapsulated the phrase. I'd let it permeate the classroom, building a culture.

This may seem overkill and perhaps even arduous, but it really works. A few weeks after I introduced our mission statements in my classroom (although the first was hidden from them), I asked the children what they represented. Here were their answers (they were seven at the time):

- we have high standards
- we try to finish best, not first
- we check for improvements
- we read aloud
- we want to have work that goes on the 'Wall of Wonder'
- we feel pride in finished work
- we want to learn and improve from the journey.

So, what was our class mantra? 'Making beautiful work'. This came from two key sources: the brilliant Pete Jones (@Pekabelo), who works as a secondary art teacher in the Channel Islands, and the story behind 'Austin's Butterfly' by Ron Berger.

Pete ran a project-based learning (PBL) scheme, nicknamed Pebble, at his school. In it, the end remit was to publicly display completed work. This involved all sorts of ingenious ideas, from public galleries to artwork and accompanying audio messages at every bus stop on his island! I loved the sheer gutsiness of his ambition, and his presentation at the #TLT15 conference demonstrated the beauty of both his students' work and his expectations. He also cited several schools who have the word 'beautiful' as part of their school aim.

I also read the story behind Austin's Butterfly. Ron Berger wrote the brilliant slim book *An Ethic of Excellence*, and the butterfly was an example of giving gentle nudges towards a finished product. The butterfly drawing was completed by a six-year-old, who had drawn it as part of a project at the school he attended, where the children's work was sold to raise money. Again, a stunningly ambitious end goal, where beautiful work is an expectation rather than a bonus for those few who manage to have neat writing or can colour in well.

Implicitly, I was suggesting, 'Can't we all produce beautiful work?' and so used this as my mission statement (which I actually call a class mantra).

The other mantra that I used – but didn't share – was to 'invite the children to learn'. There is a key difference between 'doing' work and being invited to learn something; indeed, it is something that John Hattie writes about in his book, *Visible Learning for Teachers*. In it, he states the four key skills of this as being:

- warmth
- trust
- empathy
- positive relationships.

These are four sub-values that I hold tightly to, even when planning. Rather like the public speaker who draws a smiley face on their notes to remind themselves to grin every so often, having these four key values to hand and reminding myself of them when planning, helps to nudge me to ensure that these come across not only in my teaching, but also in my interaction with the children.

Promoting core values

There is a range of ways in which this can be done; one of the most effective methods I used cost a little money but had an enormous impact. I'd spent the previous year introducing one new mantra a month. These were as follows:

- hard work feels great
- FAIL – first attempt in learning
- our deeds are our monuments

- we love to take risks
- pass on a smile inside
- we fill our life with breathtaking moments
- our age is no barrier
- from fragile to agile
- keep worries in a glass
- we read all about it
- our action guides our reaction
- nothing lasts, nothing ends, nothing is perfect
- please and thank you open doors.

These had been shared with the children in the usual way described on page 68, but also with posters, assemblies and discussions.

At the start of the summer holidays, I had a brainwave – what if I could get these values to my future students before they'd even started my class? I quickly put together a small 52-page book filled with quotes, questions and the core values themselves. I then had them printed online (about 40p a book) and sent them out to the children, to arrive by post one week before they returned to school.

The response from the parents and the children was incredible. For a start, the novelty of getting post was remarkable for some children. The buy-in from everyone was fantastic, and the parents knew exactly what I was trying to build in my classes and lessons.

Of course, this is just an example of a way in which you can get your core values across, but one that worked particularly well. You could also:

- make posters
- print stickers
- have personalised pencils made
- create a video
- emblazon them on your board
- print them for the class books.

The possibilities are virtually endless! If you do use a core value in your class, please do let me know on Twitter, using the hashtag #corevalues.

Part 4
West – planning classroom activities

Chapter 11
Pace panic

I have a simple measure for the engagement of a film. If I'm at the cinema and check my watch, it's too long or the pace is too slow. If I'm at home and end a film part-way through, it's because I'm either not engaged enough in the story or I'm too tired. It's a blunt tool, but a good measure. I have a friend who started watching a film on his way to work one day, and was so engaged that he got off at his stop, sat on the platform seating and watched through to the end!

Pace is one of those almost indefinable qualities of a lesson that cannot necessarily be put into a plan, but that can make or break a lesson. Too fast a pace and students can become confused and disengaged. Too slow a pace and students become bored and (you guessed it) disengaged. So what is the perfect pace, and how do we avoid pace panic?

Simply put, pace is the current of the learning in a lesson. It is tricky to measure and ascertain sometimes, as it has many influences: the students themselves, the materials used, the placing of the lesson, the class environment, observational issues, and so on. These are all factors in pace, and the level of the teacher's tacit knowledge in that classroom, for that subject, can alter that pace.

When the National Literacy Framework was launched in 1998 (to be taught in 1999), the literacy hour clock was published, detailing specific timings for each part of the lesson. It was both fascinating and frustrating to fit into these pockets of time within the hour, with teachers sometimes eking out some parts of the lesson and cramming in other sections within a tiny window. It gave nothing for pace apart from relentless challenge.

Luckily, we have moved away from this prescriptive time measure, but we are still mindful of rough timings for a lesson. It is difficult to place times on this when we all work to different timings for lessons but, for convenience, I have created a sample timing chart based around an hour-long lesson (with timings afterwards). Note that this is very rough, and will require professional flexibility in your thinking in order to work successfully.

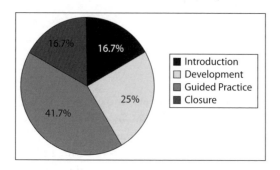

(Timing: introduction 10 minutes, development 15 minutes, guided practice 25 minutes, closure 10 minutes)

The purpose of pace is to constantly re-examine these timings on the basis of need and response – the needs of the students and the response that particular section of the lesson is getting.

The biggest danger with pace is panic. This can occur, most often within an observation, if the teacher judges the students to be drifting off in interest, or if they are aware that they have overrun a particular section.

The most important point about pace is the need to ensure that you don't race ahead if your children aren't fully on board with the stage of the lesson you are at. This makes perfect sense when you consider it. If your development aspect is overrunning because the children still haven't 'got' what they have to do, there are three things to do: stop and review where you are, carry on until they do understand, or jump on to the next task. Although the last option is the easiest to do, it is possibly the worst option to take. It is akin to driving the car out of the garage midway through a major repair – the car may run, but for how long?

From my experience, pace panic tends to choose the latter option as it appears to demonstrate lesson progress. This is true to a certain extent, but only inasmuch as it moves the lesson timing on; it doesn't necessarily move the learning along, which should be the main aim. The bravest option is to stop and review, but this takes enormous courage and guts, especially in an observed lesson. To that end, refine the skill of using 'stop and regroup' activities that you can give to the students, to allow yourself the 30 seconds you need to decide what is going wrong and how you can correct it *at this moment*.

#proplanningtip: Stop and regroup activities

These are activities and tasks you can put in at any point in a lesson to give you some breathing space and thinking time. They are short and sharp, and are time-fillers with a purpose. Almost all of them require either personal reflection or talk time.

- Turn to a partner and explain one thing you have learnt so far.
- Try to recall what we covered in the last lesson.
- What are three things you remember from our last lesson in X?
- If you were to change one thing about your learning in this lesson, what would it be?
- What do you understand so far about this topic?
- If you were to explain this idea to your parents, what would you say?

All of these questions can be used without making a dramatic dent in your lesson or the pace, and can give you a little mental sanctuary to regroup your thinking, which is often needed. More experienced teachers use this technique, often without being aware of it. Next time you have the opportunity to observe a colleague, keep an eye out for how they take mental checks while teaching. It's a really useful skill to develop, and makes you more reflective as a teacher.

Another big danger with pace is a slowing in the lesson. Primary children are, for the most part, hungry, tenacious and eager to learn. It is your responsibility to feed this hunger, and there is nothing more painful to see than a wave of boredom or indifference drifting across a class of otherwise expectant faces.

This is not to say you should be a performing or entertaining monkey – far from it. Although I would classify myself as a performance teacher, I use the enjoyment of the learning to be a strong arbiter in my pace. This is due in part to my low boredom threshold – if I am getting bored, it is highly likely that my students are too.

For more experienced teachers, the slowing of pace can be more easily identified. In general, it can lead to:

- disengaged pupils
- less participation
- noise levels changing to extremes – either incredibly quiet or loud
- misbehaviour
- laconic attitudes
- a rise in questions for supplementary reasons (increased toilet requests)
- vastly reduced attention spans
- concentration drift
- small provocations between pupils.

I'm sure you can add to this list. So how can you address this in your planning?

The easiest way is to consider each section of the lesson, and ponder how you will 'draw in' the pupils at every stage. This can be done through curiosity, excitement, anticipation, enthusiasm and something I call 'learning delight' – that joy that comes when thinking becomes aligned and the penny drops for children who have 'I get it' moments. I'll state again, these are not performance issues that an entertainer or TV presenter might use.

Curiosity – present a puzzle or question that makes the children want to find out more.

Excitement – rebrand what will happen next in the lesson as really enlightening and crucial. John Hattie in his book *Visible Learning for Teachers* calls this 'an invitation to learn', which is a beautifully-crafted phrase, encapsulating everything about engagement.

Anticipation – the carrot that drives pace and learning forward. Knowing that there is something even greater coming up soon naturally improves the pace of a lesson.

Enthusiasm – Monday morning teaching can create an enforced jollity, as can a very dry topic (adverbial phrases, anyone). Locate the passion you have for the topic, and this enthusiasm will feed through to the pupils in front of you.

Learning delight – give two or three (or more if you are able) moments when the penny drops for the children. These will be the high points of the lesson, the stages that they remember, and will also buoy up the pace considerably.

#proplanningtip: The power of stories

Time and time again when discussing this moment of 'drawing them in', the teachers I spoke to talked about three key areas – jokes and personal (related) anecdotes, short clips and films, and stories (both spoken and read out loud). I have long been sold on stories, and have found when giving a presentation to large groups of teachers and adults that stories can carry the strongest and most powerful of messages in the most memorable and accessible of formats. My largest talk so far, a keynote speech for a conference with 300 teachers in attendance, used *The Very Hungry Caterpillar* as its base.

Stories have an influence beyond simply teaching an objective or technical aspect of learning. They are somehow far more memorable than anything else you can offer, and can also help to dictate a pace, from the slow, quiet retelling of a story to calm a pace, to the edge-of-your-seat adventure to ratchet up the excitement in a lesson.

While reading stories is normally reserved for the end of the day or for English lessons, the power of a good story in any lesson can capture your children in a way that belies all other strategies. Used carefully, it can transform both the pace of your lesson and the depth of children's engagement.

There are collections of short stories you can use to illustrate points in your lesson but, from experience, the best ones to share are stories that connect you directly to the topic in question. You are far more likely to speak with interest, empathy and enticement if it is about you personally. Consider, when planning your connection to this topic, whether it is an anecdote, an experience in your life, or even a visit you have previously made to a location to which you can link. Use these, if appropriate, in your lessons. They are some of the magic.

Matching pace to need

A key principle about pace is not doing lessons faster or slower but matching the pace to the needs of the pupils. One way to monitor this is to observe your own lesson from a different perspective to your own. While there are technical tools that can help you to do this, such as IRIS Connect, one low-tech solution, however, is to film the pupils using a device such as a tablet. Set it so that it is facing the pupils and record them for a lesson you teach. Afterwards, watch that lesson – you'll see the unengaged habits appearing (see the list on page 76) if the pace dips. Different lessons need their own levels of pace, so consider the pace of a lesson when planning – it can make all the difference.

Activity essentials

While there are almost infinite numbers of activities that you can utilise to enable learning to take place in the classroom, they often follow the same skeletal formats, detailed below:

- Information through research – study around a specific topic, either by reading, discussing or exploring it in another format (think of science experiments or project research).

- Information through reveal – in essence, a match-the-job-to-the-role activity, such as identifying which body organs serve which purpose.

- Skill practice – for example, repetitive use of direct speech marks in writing, or practising formal methods of subtraction.

- Demonstration of skills/knowledge – for example, having learnt about writing features of the horror genre, children demonstrate this in a task.

Each of these serves a very specific purpose, and it can be easy to be attracted to an activity that has more appeal rather than something perhaps more functional yet which serves a better purpose.

There is an easy way to analyse your activity habits, and that is by objective slicing. This is achieved by taking a copy of some work and slicing it into three parts: the top objective, the work itself and the marking comment at the bottom. Do this for a few pieces of work and then ask another teacher in a similar age group to look at a few of these slices and, from the work, identify:

- the learning objective of the task
- whether the activity was research, retrieval, practice or demonstration.

This can help you pinpoint whether the activity and the marking are reflective of the objective itself or if there is a disconnect. They should, of course, marry up together successfully. Objective slicing is a particularly useful task to do as a year leader or phase leader, as it takes the concept of book scrutiny to more depth and can provide excellent ways to help your teachers to improve the quality of their teaching in a quick and effective manner, especially when tied in with planning.

We can be drawn as teachers to the demonstration aspect of activities more than most, but again we can employ a simple 'rule of five' to help us to ensure that this is being provided at the right stage in the learning sequence (i.e. at the end).

To that end, it really doesn't matter what activity you do, so long as it drives forwards the purpose of the objective. Clearly, you can draw on the children's interests, your passions and other determining factors, but don't let that cloud the activity purpose.

#proplanningtip: Rule of five

If children make more than five mistakes against the main objective (e.g. if the objective is to demonstrate comma use and there are fewer than five commas, or more than five commas in the wrong place), then more practice is needed to establish the concept more firmly in the students' minds.

Chapter 12
Devil's advocate: when can writing learning objectives work?

There is, of course, a key difference in a learning objective and a doing objective. If the learning objective (or LO as they are more commonly known) is stripped directly from the National Curriculum, or any curriculum you are assessing against, it can be an excellent way of referencing and evidencing progress and achievement within lessons.

Mancunian art specialist, Sophie Merrill, uses illustrated page numbers, prepared beforehand, to help her students organise their learning across themes. The same could be done for learning objectives, with teachers having a special logo for each theme they cover (e.g. a speech bubble for direct speech), with the page number inside it. This would not only allow the students to look back through their work and find a particular learning sequence quickly, but also allow a teacher to quickly trace back to identify a particular objective.

The key with writing learning objectives in books is to make them work for you rather than against you. In this sense, it would be logical to indicate what level of achievement has been made against the objective. Using either a colour or coding system works well, and it is even more successful if fed back into any data system used by the school. This, when carried out alongside marking, allows you to immediately plan your next lesson in the sequence, based on the objectives. Here is the pattern I use:

- Divide the surface of a clear desk next to where you are marking into four areas and assign a sticky note to each area. Label these according to your achievement groups. At my current school, we use working, achieved and mastered in our tracking programme. The fourth sticky note is for immediate intervention, as in 'can't wait' intervention.

- Mark each book against the objective, using the school marking scheme.
- Indicate their success against the learning objective, and put the book, closed, in the relevant pile.
- Complete the marking.
- Procrastinate a bit. This break is important, but time it!
- Enter the different groups into the tracking system. They are already grouped for you.
- Establish for your planning the next step each group needs. Write this in your planning.
- Write down your groups on your planning. This is based on your piles, and what is next in the sequence to teach.
- Update their positions on the tracking system.

This may seem long and arduous but, even as someone who is not a fan of marking, this system works brilliantly for me in covering the triumvirate of modern teaching needs: marking, assessment and planning. It does it in one fell swoop too. It also ensures that the marking and assessing are actually working for you, in that it feeds directly into planning.

I'll admit that I didn't always work this way – there was often a big gap between all these and, like any gaps, the small, important things fell through. By moving these much closer together, my marking is more focused, my assessment more accurate and my planning more beneficial. I've actually taken to assessing (and feeding into my tracker) after every lesson. This is perhaps overkill, but I feel comfortable that I can at any point define what exactly the children have covered, their achievement and where they can be placed on our school assessment grid. For the sake of integrity, I can also pinpoint evidence to back up my claims. I'm not saying it's perfect, but it's the closest I've got to a place where I feel confident in all three.

Could this still be done when not writing the learning objective? Possibly, but in terms of speed for the teacher in tracking progress, having it there works brilliantly. I know some schools use codes and other devices, but any teacher, pupil or parent can open up a book and see what was being attempted by the child if the learning objective is written down.

#proplanningtip: Marking comments

Spending your marking time, which is precious (my logic is that I teach for free and get paid for marking and planning – it's the only way I can convince myself!), simply echoing the learning objective is a BFWAT – a Big Fat Waste Of Time.

> Learning objective: To describe various 2D objects (work).
> Comment: Well done Oscar, you have described 2D objects successfully.
> Comment to teacher: Well done, you have simply underlined what you asked the child to do in the first place.
> WWW ('what worked well'): Your ability to copy words from the top of the page.
> EBI ('even better if'): You actually commented with some validity or helped with progress.

Echoing the learning objective is like Mary or Paul from the *Great British Bake Off* saying, 'Well done Oscar, you've made a Victoria sponge.' What feedback is that exactly, apart from (at a stretch) 'our eyes work'?

The best feedback in marking is to give a small, slightly uncomfortable nudge towards making the work they've produced a little better. Here is the silver bullet to enabling this, and it's not too complex. For every piece of work you mark, imagine the child sitting next to you and say to yourself: 'If you were to do this again, what small change could you make to improve it in some way?' Answer that question. It's that simple.

Ideally, you'd have the child next to you when you actually mark. This is time-consuming but transformative. This can be improved with two children next to you as you mark their work, with both watching and listening.

Guess what? This stage can be refined (yes, really) if you have the children working alongside you, rather than when they present the finished article. This is even more time-consuming (as you are essentially ignoring 28 other children at that moment), but you can see the changes as they happen. I do this in my class in what I call 'Three Minute Clinics.' One child works with me, the next in line sitting next to us, watching intently what is happening. These are the best versions of me teaching, and I've seen the greatest leaps in progress using this format. Try it once; you'll try it again, I guarantee.

Chapter 13
Lesson success criteria

So what does success look like in your classroom? Does every child know? More importantly, how do you communicate this? One phrase I often hear at the start of any teaching year is this: 'Is this enough?' This is a possible indicator of several issues:

- anchoring
- minimum effort fairy
- unconfident performance.

Anchoring

You may have anchored a specific amount of work for your students to complete, perhaps without even realising it. Any child who is told to write ten sentences using a subordinate clause but decides to write 12 just for kicks should be preserved and studied by scientists. It happens so rarely – I can think of maybe three or four children in my teaching career. Asking for a specific number of sentences or sums without any follow-on goal is a recipe for low expectations. This is essentially suggesting that they will nail the objective in that specific number of sentences. Exactly how likely is that? To my mind, this can be related to driving lessons – some learn to drive in five, others in 25. Only when the instructor is confident that you can pass do they suggest you enter for your driving test. The same should be true of teaching a specific element – it is different for everyone.

Put another way, if a child can't demonstrate a subordinate clause once in ten sentences, writing another ten sentences won't solve this problem. Far better that you assess after five sentences. This is why I use 'I tick the block' in many lessons. Put simply, the children start on a task, with the requirement that they check with me after the first block of work – be it the first three sentences, the first row of sums, whatever the task is. This allows me to quickly see that they get the concept, and ensures that I can guide them on the right path if they are confused. It also helps me to counter the 'theory of knowledge' (the disparity between what the teacher thinks children have learnt and what they've actually learnt). If more than five children are making the same mistake, I pause work and remedy the misconception. The time cost of doing this outweighs a class plodding through work incorrectly. This is the essence of teaching.

Minimum effort fairy

This is the equivalent of a microwave meal – it qualifies as food, but is entirely without effort. Often, if a child isn't invited into the learning or invested in the concept ('Does this have any benefit for me?'), they will produce the bare minimum – enough to get the ticks needed – and move on to something more interesting.

This can be challenged with a line of effort. Draw a line under the work, with a bold dot to the left and an arrow at the right end of the line. Ask the child to describe the task at the very end of the effort line. What would it look like? They are able to do this with ease (and a little training).

Now ask them to place their work on this line. Highlight the disparity (there will be one if they are honest, but they may need some guidance at first). Under this disparity, write down three things that could be improved. Set them back to task.

Unconfident performance

We all have children in classes who are plagued with self-doubt, with 'plague' being the right term. They question their effort in everything, and worry that what they have done is simply not enough.

This is the most delicate situation to deal with in response to 'Is this enough?' and should be handled with extreme care. This is the one time when the 'tickled pink' highlighter really works wonders. Go through their work, highlighting the very best parts of what they have achieved so far, while subtly giving small tips for improvement. Note, these should be small nudges rather than a message akin to 'You really haven't got this at all, have you?' (and if you genuinely think this, it's on you as their teacher rather than them as a learner – sorry).

After your feedback, highlight the next three lines in the margin, and ask them to continue in the same (or an improved) vein.

Demonstrating excellent success criteria can be carried out in a number of ways, outlined in the following chapter (see page 89).

Chapter 14
Outrageous expectations

The geeks at Google call this 'moonshot thinking', but I also like Hywel Robert's use of 'imagineering' – imagine the best outcome and engineer it backwards to Earth. I've always found that having a genuine audience for work is the best way to mark out expectations. If children are creating a page for a non-fiction book, make the expectation that this page could *actually end up in a book*. Unrealistic? Possibly, but if you have that aim, the expectations are subtly raised away from scrappy handwriting and bubble titles.

I have in the past held galleries of work (CD album cases), had books printed for the class (expensive but, as a print fetishist, totally worth it) or recorded and uploaded to SoundCloud (think YouTube for audio, but faster and easier, and with far less hassle in terms of pupil anonymity). We've also written reviews of books and submitted them to Amazon (enormously satisfying), written letters to companies (FREE STUFF – seriously) and contacted authors via Twitter (utter win – I've never *not* had a response from a living author). One child's photo achieved second place in a photography competition. Work out the best end point at which any piece of work could realistically be placed, and work back from that – the reward for the children alone is enormous.

Portfolios of excellence

One practice I set up in a previous school was for each subject to have a portfolio of excellence. In it, the subject leader took in fantastic work from their subject as and when it appeared. It was good to have this folder of evidence, but it really came into its own in subsequent years when, through osmosis, teachers began using it to define expectations with the students. Not only did this help with planning (as an end point to work back from), but it also gave the children a very valuable benchmark – someone your age, in this lesson, could produce *this*.

Learning journey

This is similar to portfolios of excellence – typically carried out in Early Years, although some schools are adopting this for all their pupils, collating the best piece of work in English and maths each half term. As someone who recently found his old junior school books, this will have enormous sentimental value for pupils. The company now offers digital Learning Journeys for 3-11 year olds. Using it allows you to track and evidence examples of work, as well as producing clear packages for parents to look at. It is also incredibly good value, especially if it replaces teachers carefully printing out colour photos, cutting these out and sticking them into scrap books.

Visualiser goodness

From my limited exposure to them, visualisers tend to be used in plenaries and sometimes lesson starters. I think that they are exceptional for use during the lesson to show successful ongoing work. They are a quick and very visual marker for expectations – you are able to say 'this is what I am looking for; this is successful learning' to the whole class in seconds.

This year is the first year I've had a visualiser, and I have to say I'm a little bit in love with it – enough to commit to saying that I think that it's one of the best technological advances in classrooms after the overhead projector (and not the interactive whiteboard). I love that I can demonstrate something intricate on a massive scale. This was highlighted to me when I first used it to teach centimetres and millimetres. I was able to show how I measured an actual line, using an actual ruler. Lots of software can recreate a ruler, but nothing – *nothing* – beats using the primary tool. I recently saw a Year 6 teacher teaching angles using software with a protractor. I wanted to leap in and say, 'Use your visualiser!' but I didn't. I did suggest it afterwards.

A final wish for technologists – invent one that I can use hands-free, walking around the classroom. I've tried with an iPad, and it just isn't the same.

Hold and show

This is low-rent, low-effort and, frankly, low-impact, but having a child hold up their work for others to quickly see works well as a ten-second expectation intervention. It works best as a layout guide, especially for presentation. It has a very strong immediate response, however. Do this at the start of a written task, and watch how many children grab a ruler.

Wall of Wonder

Since naming it the 'Wall of Wonder', I've subsequently discovered, teaching dinosaur that I am, that these are often called 'working walls'. Never mind, the Wall of Wonder solves many ills in my classroom, and can for you too.

When work is complete, ask the children if they think it is good enough for the WoW. If you both agree, announce this to the class and Blu-Tack™ it up (or use magnets if you wish). It allows other children to see the standard and expectation you'd most like to witness in class, and is crazily motivational for the children – they love it. Reward doesn't have to be stickers and smiley faces – in fact, careful, directed and public praise can be the best, quickest and most effective form of reward for almost any child. I read once that the body releases a chemical when hugged for longer than eight seconds, so I always try to make a praise statement last at least eight seconds or not at all. Before you worry for my class, they implicitly know this. Throwaway praise is hollow and purposeless. Try this next time you have to say thank you to someone: precede it with 'hey' and get their eye contact, and then thank them. The difference is enormous.

Success criteria statements

Many primary schools are heading towards more formalised demonstrations of success criteria, through tick lists, scales for improvement or statements to match children's learning against. My favourite of all these is something incredibly clever I saw a student teacher carry out. In my current school, we use phases of learning, where we define introductory, independent, emerging and mastery statements for the children to measure themselves against. These are commonly shown to the class and talked through, but what my student did was to blend them into one understandable statement, colour-coded to show the different phases within the statement:

> *I will confidently solve complex subtraction sums using formal methods.*
> *I will check my work using mental strategies and inverse sums.*

This would be a sample explanatory spiel to accompany the statement:

> *Everyone should by the end of this week be able to solve subtraction sums.*
> *I know that this will be easier for some of you than others, and hope that*
> *everyone will become more confident with using formal methods, although of*
> *course you can make notes and manipulatives – I hope that by showing you*
> *this method, you'll find it the easiest way. I know some of you will also be*
> *able to check your work using simple mental strategies, and others will use*
> *inverse sums to ensure every sum is right.*

This would be said while pointing through the key words and phrases, and I have found that it helps in two key ways. It firstly clarifies for you exactly what you are looking for. It also explains the rate of learning and areas covered for the children. It's a win–win strategy, and provides a good place to judge learning upon during the sequence of lessons.

When should you show the success criteria? I believe, if possible, it should be available throughout the lesson. It's an easy method for a child to be able to check the criteria against their work and ensure that they are on-task within the sequence. A short conversation with them about their work in relation to the success criteria can help both of you unpick the areas of future focus. In reality, of course, it more commonly appears at the beginning and end of lessons, which is a step in the right direction. Hidden success criteria can result in children losing direction of 'what is expected' beyond simply delivering answers.

#proplanningtip: Wintervention

This is a term and system devised by myself and my brilliant TA, through an ongoing discussion about how to feed back as quickly as possible to children in order to correct them from their learning tangent.

We use a range of strategies to do this. One builds on the relationship we have together in the classroom. If I am teaching and a child is struggling, I'll either say their name to my TA as a flag, or I'll ask two children to swap, so that the child moved near her gets help. This is implicit in the move, and everyone knows the reason and is comfortable with it.

Likewise, after every spelling test, I give my TA the score list and a cut-off line. She'll then work on that specific spelling sound with the children above that line.

If children are ill, a partner will stick in any work in their book, write in any objective, and then put the book on my TA's desk. She knows then that they need to catch up, and will help them to do so in those stolen minutes during the day.

Wintervention works brilliantly because of our relationship. It has untold benefits for the class, and I'd like to thank my long-suffering TA in print for her tolerance of my ideas, whims and poor-quality jokes.

Chapter 15
The scourge of learning admin

This has to be one of my biggest pet hates, even above using inadequate worksheets. Learning admin has bugged me for years, mainly because it is like biting one's nails; you are aware it may be a bad habit, but it is hard to stop unless you take direct action.

Learning admin is easily defined as an activity that looks busy or like learning, but isn't really. This was much more eloquently described by Professor Rob Coe in his 2013 presentation *From Evidence to Great Teaching*, where he called such tasks (with far more gravitas) poor proxies for learning. Here is his list:

Poor proxies for learning (easily observed, but not really about learning):

1. students are busy: lots of work is done (especially written work)

2. students are engaged, interested, motivated

3. students are getting attention: feedback, explanations

4. classroom is ordered, calm, under control

5. curriculum has been 'covered' (i.e. presented to students in some form)

6. (at least some) students have supplied correct answers (whether or not they really understood them or could reproduce them independently).

We've all seen these, either in our classroom, or in other classrooms. Posters, dice use, word searches and, to a certain extent, group work can all come under the category of learning admin.

Let's explore an example. It's a favourite of mine, only because it highlights clearly where the holes are.

For the past few days, your class have been learning column addition. To mix it up, you ask them to generate their own sums using dice. They love it! The classroom is lively and abuzz with noise and maths in action.

At the end of the lesson, you look at their books. Some children managed nine or ten sums. That seems fewer than you'd hoped for. You then consider that they had a whole hour (minimal input from you at this stage in the sequence), meaning that each sum took six minutes to record. Let's consider what actually happened in the lesson:

- dice were played with, argued over and swapped
- the pencils were picked up and put down – a lot
- layouts were adjusted
- some addition happened.

Despite the appearance of being incredibly cool with a fulfilled life, I'm actually quite sad, so I once timed this activity, recording what was going on. An addition sum took three minutes and seven seconds to generate and complete. Of that, 21 seconds were spent calculating the answer.

21 seconds. Or, to put it another way, 11.2% of the time the task took was devoted to the actual learning objective. That isn't due to a lack of commitment – which, to me, is learning *neglect*. You couldn't justify that percentage to parents or governors, so how come it happens in class so frequently?

I think it links back to the poor proxies examples. Good learning admin looks suspiciously so much like proper learning, it can hardly be recognised. It's the reverse of disguised learning. That is the scary part. The not-scary news is that it's really easy to detect if you ask the right question, which is: 'Is what the children are doing at each stage helping them to achieve the objective?'

Let's look at an example to work through with this in mind.

The learning objective: Learn to use a subordinate clause correctly

There are countless activities with which to tackle this challenge. You could have some jigsaw sentences to match up and then stick in. their books You could ask the children to write some sentences containing subordinate clauses. You could get them to identify the subordinate clause in a string of sentences. All of these have value.

If we look at the objective more carefully, however, we can see that perhaps these have been taught before, so are familiar but not fully understood, given the use of the word *correctly*. We also need to focus on the verb *use*. Let's examine those activities again.

Jigsaw sentences – this activity can be useful for helping children identify main and subordinate clauses, but it doesn't help the children use them. They are merely matching up the most suitable ones, so the skill they are using is finding the clue in each that joins them up.

Write sentences – this is a stock activity but, again, the main focus isn't subordinate clauses but inventing content. If you are unsure, set one child this task and time how much energy is expended on the subordinate clause work, and how much is spent on creating content. You'd be surprised. For the inventive child, this is perfect and not a problem at all, but this isn't most children in your class.

Identify the subordinate clause – any activity that involves highlighting or underlining is most suited as a starter or plenary activity, to be honest. A quick way to test this is imagining a child entering your lesson halfway through. If you can explain what they have to do in under 30 seconds and they can complete it without your input, is it really a valid main task activity? It also uses the verb *identify* rather than *use*.

Here is what I might do in this situation: give out a sheet, with a range of sentences, some with the main clause missing, others with the subordinate clause missing. Because I know most subordinate clauses can be found in the middle or at the end of sentences, I would vary their location. I know that this would involve some creativity, but it would also require careful thought, and children would have a topic provided by the part clue in each sentence. If I was going to do 100% clean learning, I'd have the children writing directly onto the sheet, since copying sentences off a sheet and into a book is – well – copying, not using.

Learning admin is easy to remove, but does provide more work for you to do if you are really strict. The benefit is that the children are far more likely to get to the learning destination accurately and quickly this way. Think of it as a leisurely drive to your holiday compared to taking the direct route – less pretty but more efficient!

IN PRACTICE: Carry out an audit of the work completed by your class last week. What could you have changed to make it more efficient? Was there any learning admin that you could identify? Was the learning aim explicit in everything the children did? This last question is easy to test – get the work, cover the objective and ask a teaching colleague in another year group to guess the objective, with as much clarity as possible. If they can't, what hope do your children have?

Some teachers might object to this, saying that the children need breathing space in activities, that this type of 'filleting' removes creativity and is quite robotic. I would robustly challenge this. By ensuring that the children can successfully use subordinate clauses, they are more likely to have the confidence to actually *use* them in creative writing. It is front-loading skills teaching. Given the right approach of inviting the children to learn, explaining the benefits of learning new techniques and refining existing ones, as well as practising key skills, only enhances creativity later on – it's rather like being taught what those mysterious icons do on an illustration program such as Photoshop. Yes, it might take time, but the long-term benefits are enormous.

Chapter 16
Online worksheets

I hold my hands up, I use a worksheet that I have downloaded online at least once a week. I tend to use TES Resources, Primary Resources and a few others, and you can also get a subscription to companies like Twinkl, which do a great job at specific worksheets. The web addresses for these are given in the References and recommended reading section at the end of the book (see page 107).

There is, however, an enormous danger in using online worksheets straight off (as in, downloading them, printing them and using them without any changes) and it is in the 'close enough' mentality. This danger can befall us all; we start with a learning objective, think it would be easier to search for some activity online than to create your own bespoke activity, and then begin the big search. Five minutes and several failed downloads later, we find something that is 75% successful against our objectives, and so we print this out to use.

It is at this point that you have compromised your objectives. What might happen, which is worse, is that you might even skew your teaching to have this worksheet as the end point. Suddenly, your objective is off the rails, heading in a distinctly different direction to the one that you had planned. It's akin to planning a pork meal, discovering that there are no pork joints and buying a chicken instead – it's a different meal!

I have a rule of thumb when using online resources – I'll stop searching after the first three unsuccessful hits. If you can't find something in the first 90 seconds, why not make it yourself? I'll also customise it for my class if need be. If it detracts from my objective, I won't use it. If it makes me change my input, I won't use it. If it uses Comic Sans. . . well, you get the picture.

#proplanningtip: Sharing online

Despite what may seem like online resource bashing, I'm actually a huge advocate of sharing activities, worksheets and resources online. In 2013, I calculated (very roughly, I might add, fact pedants) that each teacher on average shares just under half a lesson's worth of resources each year online. Isn't that some kind of madness? Each Sunday, around 30,000 of us will probably be planning essentially the same lessons, and then creating 30,000 resources! If we all donated the resources from just one day of teaching the entire year, there would be over 8 million items to choose from online – wouldn't that be incredible?

Of course, that won't happen; the majority of resources are donated by a very small minority of teachers. But why not make it a pledge to donate just one resource each half term – something that really made a difference in your classroom?

Here's an example. Early in 2016, I realised that the children in my class were desperate for a job. This isn't uncommon, but I wasn't happy with any format of job identifier I'd seen in schools or online. One evening it came to me: a dusty memory of a cipher wheel – two alphabets inside each other to make a code. A bit of designing and I'd made my job wheel, where each child had a job and the wheel rotated one place each day. I took a picture of it and put it online. It was seen over 5,000 times in one week, with 500 people interested in it. The method for sharing an idea or activity online is so easy now, you really should consider it. Go to the online resources for the book at www.bloomsbury.com/lockyer-lesson-planning to find the job wheel for you to use.

Appendix

The following flow charts have been designed to help teachers understand the interwoven nature of planning, teaching, marking and assessing. The best planning I carry out occurs at the same time as I mark, and these charts will help to remind you of the core purposes and functions of each stage.

Think of these as a mental tick list. I have used them to support colleagues who are stuck on a particular stage, and in refining my own thinking on the relationship between (for example) marking and assessing, which are two distinct skills.

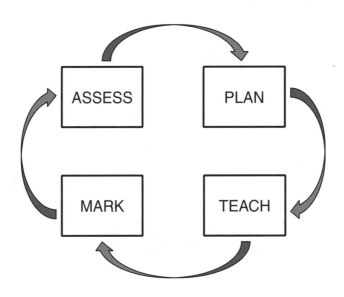

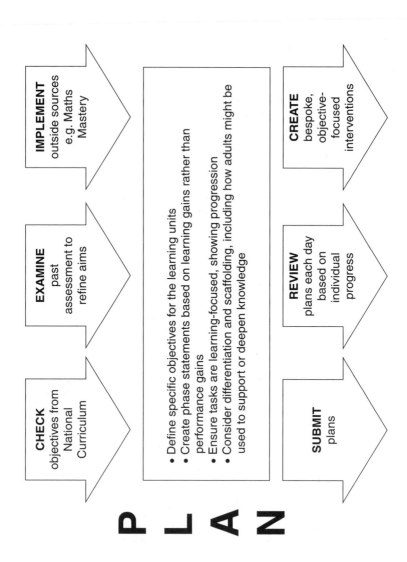

IMPLEMENT outside sources e.g. Maths Mastery

EXAMINE past assessment to refine aims

CHECK objectives from National Curriculum

PLAN

- Define specific objectives for the learning units
- Create phase statements based on learning gains rather than performance gains
- Ensure tasks are learning-focused, showing progression
- Consider differentiation and scaffolding, including how adults might be used to support or deepen knowledge

CREATE bespoke, objective-focused interventions

REVIEW plans each day based on individual progress

SUBMIT plans

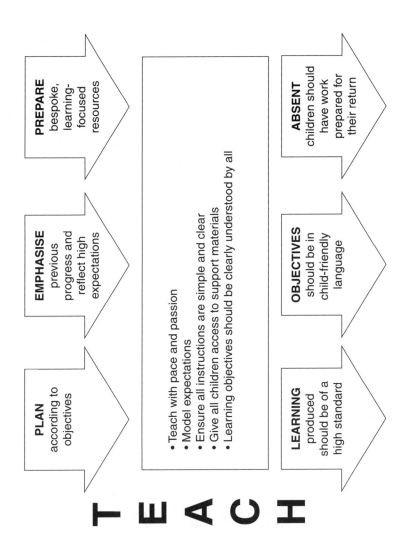

T

PLAN
according to
objectives

EMPHASISE
previous
progress and
reflect high
expectations

PREPARE
bespoke,
learning-
focused
resources

E
A
C

• Teach with pace and passion
• Model expectations
• Ensure all instructions are simple and clear
• Give all children access to support materials
• Learning objectives should be clearly understood by all

H

LEARNING
produced
should be of a
high standard

OBJECTIVES
should be in
child-friendly
language

ABSENT
children should
have work
prepared for
their return

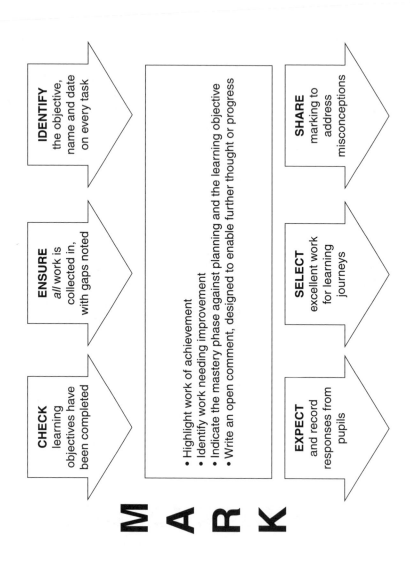

M
A
R
K

CHECK learning objectives have been completed

ENSURE *all* work is collected in, with gaps noted

IDENTIFY the objective, name and date on every task

- Highlight work of achievement
- Identify work needing improvement
- Indicate the mastery phase against planning and the learning objective
- Write an open comment, designed to enable further thought or progress

EXPECT and record responses from pupils

SELECT excellent work for learning journeys

SHARE marking to address misconceptions

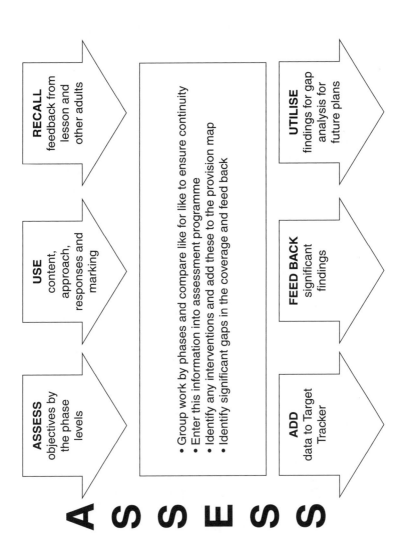

ASSESS objectives by the phase levels

USE content, approach, responses and marking

RECALL feedback from lesson and other adults

- Group work by phases and compare like for like to ensure continuity
- Enter this information into assessment programme
- Identify any interventions and add these to the provision map
- Identify significant gaps in the coverage and feed back

ADD data to Target Tracker

FEED BACK significant findings

UTILISE findings for gap analysis for future plans

A S S E S S

References and recommended reading

Berger, R. (2003), *An Ethic of Excellence: Building a Culture of Craftsmanship with Students*. Portsmouth: Heinemann.

Coe, R. et al. (2014), 'What makes great teaching? Review of the underpinning research'. The Sutton Trust. www. suttontrust. com.

Coe, R. (2015), *From Evidence to Great Teaching*. ASCL Annual Conference, Durham University.

DfE (2013), *Geography programmes of study: key stages 1 and 2*. Crown copyright.

Dudley, P. (2011) 'Lesson Study development in England: from school networks to national policy', *International Journal for Lesson and Learning Studies*, 1.1: 85–100.

Carle, E. (1987), *The Very Hungry Caterpillar*. New York, NY: Philomel Books.

Hattie, J. (2012), *Visible Learning for Teachers: Maximizing Impact on Learning*. Routledge.

Lemov, D. (2011), *Teach Like a Champion, 62 Techniques that Put Students on the Path to College*. John Wiley & Sons.

Lockyer, S. (2015), *100 Ideas for Primary Teachers: Outstanding Teaching*. Bloomsbury.

Lockyer, S. (2015), *Hands Up: Questions to Ignite Thinking in the Classroom*. Teacherly.

Lockyer, S. (2015), *Thinking about Thinking: Learning Habits Explored*. Teacherly.

Watterson, B. (1988), *The Essential Calvin and Hobbes*: a Calvin and Hobbes Treasury. Andrews and McMeel Publishing.

Wiseman, R. (2010), *59 Seconds: Think a Little, Change a Lot*. Pan Macmillan.

Zimmerman, B. J. and Schunk, D. H. (2011), *Handbook of Self-regulation of Learning and Performance*. Taylor & Francis.

Websites

All the links below, as well as the cipher and job wheels, are available on the companion website for the book, found at: www.bloomsbury.com/lockyer-lesson-planning.

5 minute lesson plan: www.teachertoolkit.me/the-5-minute-lesson-plan

Dudley, P. (2011), Lesson Study: a handbook, http://lessonstudy.co.uk/wp-content/uploads/2012/03/Lesson_Study_Handbook_-_011011-1.pdf

Hywel Roberts' blog: www.createlearninspire.co.uk

Primary resources: www.primaryresources.co.uk

Teacher Development Trust: tdtrust.org

TES teaching resources: www.tes.com/teaching-resources

Twinkl: www.twinkl.co.uk

Zappos core values: www.zappos.com/core-values

Index